Windows of Faith

Pam Rhodes

Windows of FAITH

Inspiring personal
stories of ***God's amazing grace***

Pam Rhodes

3ABN books

Pacific Press®
Publishing Association
Nampa, Idaho | Oshawa, Ontario, Canada
www.pacificpress.com

Cover and Inside Layout and Design: Chrystique Neibauer | cqgraphicdesign.com
Editor: Brenda Walsh
Copy Editor: Mellisa Hoffman
Cover Images: shutterstock.com
Cover Image: Robert Copeland

Unless otherwise noted, the author is solely responsible for the photos inside this book.

The author assumes full responsiblity for the accuracy of all quotations and facts as cited in this book.

Additional copies of this book are available from:

Adventist Book Centers®: Call toll-free 1-800-765-6955 or visit www.adventistbookcenter.com.

3ABN: Call (618) 627-4651 or visit www.store.3abn.org.

3ABN Books is dedicated to bringing you the best in published materials consistent with the mission of Three Angels Broadcasting Network. Our goal is to uplift Jesus Christ through books, audio, and video materials by our family of 3ABN presenters. Our in-depth Bible study guides, devotionals, biographies, and lifestyle materials promote whole person health and the mending of broken people. For more information, call 618-627-4651 or visit 3ABN's Web site: www.3ABN.org.

Visit Pam and Jimmy Rhodes on the Web at www.pamandjimmyrhodes.com.

ISBN 13: 978-0-8163-4458-1
ISBN 10: 0-8163-4458-2

13 14 15 16 17 • 5 4 3 2 1

Dedication

I lovingly dedicate this book to my heavenly Father, the Monarch of the universe, who still bends down to be my dearest, most precious Friend! He has walked with me all my life, and as some of these stories portray, He has protected me and guided my every step. It is my heart's desire that His name be glorified! As you read this book, I hope you'll be convinced that He is loving, gentle, and full of mercy. He is my Savior and He is yours too, if you will accept Him for what He's done for you.

I also dedicate this book to my loving husband, Jimmy. I would have never written a word without his unending encouragement! He is my best friend and a loving companion. He is also one of the most talented musicians I know. The music ministry that we've shared has kept us very close to each other and to Christ. God truly blessed me when He gave me Jimmy!

Table of Contents

Foreword

The hand of God is mighty. In the little situations of daily life, as well as the events that overwhelm, He is there, ready to reach out and save. So often, we are unaware of the protection, guidance, and help that angels provide until we look back and realize that it could never have happened without the hand of God. In this book, you will see how God has stepped in and touched the lives of a family. At times, when it looked impossible, He was there. When life itself was endangered, He was there. When they just needed to be encouraged, He was there. These stories will increase your faith as you see how, in the ordinary trials of everyday life, God met their needs and let them know He loved and cared for them.

I have known Pam Rhodes and her family since she was a teenager in my church in Albuquerque, New Mexico. I was impressed with her desire and willingness to help, as well as her devotion to God, which has continued to this day. As teachers and musicians, she and her husband, Jimmy, have ministered to thousands of people in word and song, sharing the wonderful hope and assurance we have in Christ Jesus. Your heart will rejoice as you read how God opened the *Windows of Faith* and let in the blessings of heaven.

—Kenneth Cox

With Special Thanks

To my editor, Brenda Walsh, for your suggestions, guidance, and for seeing this project through. You are so gifted and I admire how tirelessly you work for the Lord. I am amazed that you would take the time out of your incredibly busy schedule to help me! You've become a dear and treasured friend, and I cherish the times when we just sit and giggle!

Thanks, also, to your staff, Mellisa Hoffman and Chrystique Neibauer, who helped edit and format this book. They are two talented ladies that I've enjoyed getting to know! You've all been such an incredible blessing!

Overalls on Fire

The assembly of the wicked have inclosed me: they pierced my hands and feet. Psalm 22:16, KJV

"Now children, what are you supposed to do if your clothes catch on fire?" the fireman asked the children in my classroom.

"STOP, DROP, AND ROLL!" the first- and second-graders responded enthusiastically.

Stop, drop, and roll, I thought to myself. *If only someone had taught my mother to do that. It might have saved her from being burned so badly!*

My mother, June, was the third eldest of seven children. She loved all her siblings, but she especially adored her two older brothers, Clyde and Scott, and tried hard to keep up with them. If one of them climbed a tree, skipped rocks, or took a swim in the pond, she would do it right along with them. I'm sure, to her brothers, she was an annoying little tag-a-long, but June considered herself "one of the guys"!

On one particular Sunday afternoon, Scott was given the task of raking the leaves in the front yard into big piles and then burning them.

"This will take all day," he muttered under his breath. Scott was not at all happy about the job he had been given, since he had already made his own plans for the weekend, and it didn't include raking leaves! Of course, my mother, who was about six years old, was excited to help her big brother.

Scott handed June a rake and put her to work. He showed her how to rake the leaves into big piles.

"Call me when your piles are large enough, and I'll burn them," he instructed.

It wasn't long before several fires were started, and little June continued to rake. It was a beautiful fall day with a hint of a breeze blowing gently through the trees. She was enjoying every minute *helping* her big brother.

Then suddenly, without warning, one of her pant legs burst into flames! She screamed for Scott and quickly started to remove her overalls. Scott looked across the yard and, sensing what she was about to do, yelled, "Don't take your clothes off, someone might see you!"

Terrified and not knowing what else to do, June began running toward the house as fast as she could, screaming at the top of her lungs! Of course, by running, she was doing the opposite of what she should have done! In those days, no one was teaching fire safety and the importance of *Stop, drop, and roll!*

She made a beeline for the front porch. She was almost ready to open the door when she suddenly remembered her mother's rule. She and her brothers were not allowed to use the front door. They must enter and exit from the back door only. Mother had established this rule in hopes of keeping the parlor clean.

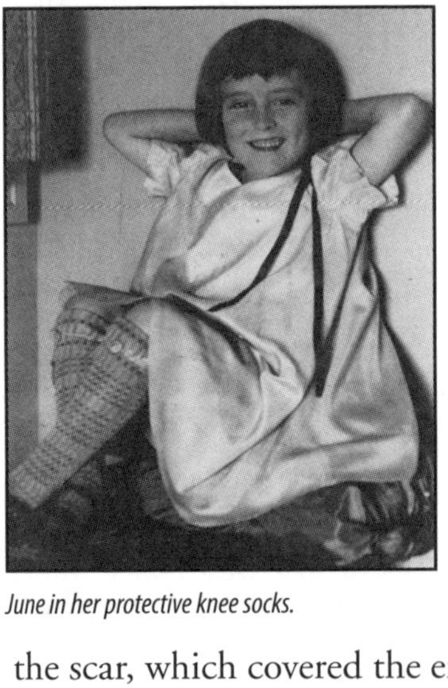

June in her protective knee socks.

Screaming and crying, she ran to the back door where Hattie, their housekeeper, quickly put out the fire. Hattie then rubbed butter all over her leg, which made it hurt even more. At that time, it was considered the best remedy, and they didn't know it was the worst treatment for a burn!

It took a long time for my mother's leg to heal, and during this time she wore knee socks to protect the new tender skin. Long after her wounds had healed, she continued to wear those long socks to hide the awful scar.

I was just a child when I asked her about the scar, which covered the entire front of her right leg. I felt so sad for her because she was such a beautiful woman and didn't deserve to have such an ugly, scarred leg. I also felt anger toward Uncle Scott for not doing more to help her, although I'm sure he just didn't know what to do.

I will say this for my mother: she never made a big deal about it or harbored any resentment toward Scott. She just took the whole thing in stride. In fact, she got a job as a lifeguard at a local swimming pool in her town when she was eighteen. She did, however, get really upset with me when I burned MY leg on the manifold of a motorcycle! I'll never forget her remark, "I guess you and I weren't meant to have pretty legs!"

As I write this story, I'm reminded of the Harry Anderson painting of the little girl sitting on Jesus' lap. She's pointing to the Savior's hands, as if to ask how He got the scars. Jesus knows about pain and suffering. He knew what He was getting Himself into when He came to die for our sins. His pain was much more than anything we will ever be asked to bear, because He felt that He was forever separated from His Father. He couldn't see life beyond the tomb and yet, He was willing to die so that we could live! But the Bible tells us that God was there and knew what His Son was going through. The Bible tells us in Psalm 22:24, "For He has not despised nor abhorred the affliction of the afflicted; nor has He hidden His face from Him; but when He cried to Him, He heard" (NKJV). What a marvelous Savior! The King of the universe wants to lead and guide us. He wants us to live with Him forever!

Friend, are you suffering with physical or emotional pain that is more than you can bear? Are you longing for someone to care and someone to help? Jesus knows and understands your situation, and He has the scars to prove it. Tell Him all about it, and ask Him to carry your burdens and to give you His peace that passes all understanding.

My Brother "Bubby"

Be kindly affectionate to one another with brotherly love, in honor giving preference to one another. Romans 12:10, NKJV

If I were to choose the person who influenced me the most spiritually as a child, it would definitely be my older brother, Carol Blake, who I affectionately called "Bubby." I called him "Bubby" from the first moment I could talk, and in my heart, he has been "Bubby" to me ever since. When he was attending La Sierra College, my family and I went out to visit him. He was showing us around and introducing us to some of his friends, when I slipped up and called him "Bubby" in front of everybody! Poor guy, he just about never lived that one down!

Pam and her brother, Bubby, at the piano.

The Lord gave Carol Blake a tremendous gift of music. He not only could read music but he played by ear as well. He started playing the piano and organ for church when he was very young. When I was three years old, he discovered that I could sing. By age five, he had coaxed me up front, singing for church. Many times he would remind me that whenever I agreed to sing, I couldn't back out at the last minute! He wanted to make sure that I understood the importance of making a commitment and keeping my word. I would always promise him that I would not back down. Weeks before I was to sing, he would patiently practice the song with me over and over again, making sure I knew every word. But sadly, much to my brother's disappointment, there were times that the night before I was scheduled to sing, I became so frightened that I would chicken out! Poor Bubby! He was such a patient brother, because he never gave up on me!

One time when I was singing, I forgot the words and stopped right in the middle of the song. Carol Blake was playing the piano and when I stopped, he began to sing until he got me back on track. Sometimes I would be so embarrassed that I would burst out in tears and just run off the platform!

Because of my brother's love and unbelievable patience, I have a wonderful music ministry today. Along with my husband, Jimmy, I do concerts across the country and via television on Three Angels Broadcasting Network, around the world. I'm happiest when I'm singing for Jesus!

There are many stories about my brother, Carol Blake, that I could share with you that would reveal his Christian character. But this one is a favorite memory. You see, my family loved to go to Red River, New Mexico, each year to ride horses. It was something that we all loved to do. But this particular year, my mother broke the news that our trip would be canceled because Carol Blake was having his wisdom teeth removed. My younger brother, Ron, and I groaned and complained when we heard the news! What? Not go to Red River! Why, that would be horrible!

Bubby, knowing how disappointed we were, convinced our mother that he would be fine and to please not cancel the trip. I still remember how sad I felt watching Bubby bravely riding his horse, trying not to show that he was miserable and in terrible pain. My precious brother was simply demonstrating the love God's Word tells us about in Romans 12:10. He unselfishly put the desires of his sister and brother above his own needs—just like Jesus did. Oh, that we would all strive to be more like Jesus!

Bubby and Pam.

Carol Blake helped develop my musical talent for the Lord, but more importantly, he is the one who introduced me to Jesus. He taught me about heaven, and how I could go there by simply accepting Christ as my Lord and Savior. He told me how much Jesus loved me and died to save me. My brother was studying for the ministry, and when he came home for vacations, he would sit with me on the front porch and as we looked up into the night sky, adorned with sparkling stars, he would share with me what he had learned in school. It is because of the unconditional love my brother showed me—and his faithful, Christian witness—that I dedicated my life to the Lord.

Dear friend, do you wish you had someone in your life that loved you unconditionally and put your happiness above his own? The good news is . . . you do! Jesus is always there for you and loves you so much that He gave His life for you. He willingly gave His life on that rugged cross and endured a painful death so that you and I might have eternal life. He loves you with an everlasting love! Run to Him! He is your Savior who is waiting with arms outstretched wide!

The Candied Apple

A merry heart does good like medicine,
but a broken spirit dries the bones. Proverbs 17:22, NKJV

The Bible tells us that we should be happy. How can we not be happy, when we have the Lord in our hearts? Not only should we be happy, but I think we should see the humorous side of life. The purpose of this story is to do nothing more than, hopefully, make you laugh.

It was gorgeous in Santa Fe, New Mexico, and our family was enjoying a day of sightseeing. I was just a little girl and my big brother, Carol Blake, who was a teenager, was pushing my baby brother, Ron, in a stroller. We were walking around the square of old, historic Santa Fe where the Indians had their handmade blankets spread out along the walk and were busy selling their silver and turquoise jewelry.

This was their peak season, so there were street vendors everywhere. Delicious aromas filled the air. People were standing in line to buy cotton candy, fried tortillas, and just about everything you could want from burritos to ice cream. Carol Blake spotted a vendor who was selling candied apples, one of his favorite treats. My mother spotted a cute, little boutique, one of her favorite treats! So she bought Carol a candied apple and asked him to stay right outside the front of the store to eat it. He was to also watch my little brother and me while she went inside to look around.

Carol really enjoyed eating his candied apple, so crisp and gooey. But when he had eaten about half of it, it wasn't so good anymore! He knew if he took even one more bite, he would be sick. So he looked for a trash can to dump what was left of his apple. There wasn't one anywhere. Suddenly, while facing the store that Mother had gone into, he noticed a mannequin in the window. She was positioned near the front door. One hand was on her hip and the other hand was gesturing with the palm side up. It looked as if her hand formed a cup. Carol Blake suddenly got this mischievous look on his face. He carefully looked to the right and then to the left, then quietly sneaked into the store, and quickly placed the candied apple, apple side down, into the mannequin's hand! He then raced out of the store and began to run as fast as he could go, pushing the stroller while making sure that I kept up with his pace.

When he reached the end of the block, he stopped, half hiding behind the edge of a building. He and I both watched as my mother came out of the store. All I could think about was how funny that mannequin looked holding that half-eaten candied apple and how my brother was going to be grounded for life!

Mother came out of the store and looked up and down the block but didn't see us anywhere. Then she slowly turned back toward the front of the store. Her eyes grew wide and her mouth went into the biggest grin. She finally just busted out laughing!

Since she seemed to enjoy the whole prank as much as Carol Blake did, he waved his arms over his head, letting her know our whereabouts.

You're probably asking if my brother got punished. Knowing my mother, I'm sure he did. I don't remember, I was too little. All I remember was my brother doing something silly and all of us having a wonderful time.

Do you enjoy life? Do people want to be around you because you're happy and positive even though we live in this tired old world of sin? I think one of the greatest witnesses we can give is to put forth a joyful and happy disposition, especially to our children. I love it when I run into former students and they tell me what a funny teacher I was and how they learned better when they laughed. So lighten up! And enjoy your walk with the Lord.

The Ugliest Angel

*"Man looks at the outward appearance,
but the* Lord *looks at the heart." 1 Samuel 16:7, NKJV*

That is the ugliest kid I have ever seen! I thought to myself. I was eight years old and my family was enjoying a working vacation in Phoenix, Arizona. Dad was there on business and, while he worked, my mom, two brothers, and I enjoyed the swimming pool at the motel.

My older brother, Carol Blake, was sixteen and I idolized him. He was always so sweet to me and took me everywhere he went, even when he was with his friends. I'm sure, if he were honest, hanging out with his little sister and baby brother was not his idea of a real vacation! But as always, he was patient and good to us.

As a tiny child, I prayed that I could have a little brother, and until he was born, I had an imaginary brother that I named Ronnie. He went with me everywhere. One day my grandfather came to take me somewhere, and as he was helping me into his car, I told him not to forget Ronnie. So my grandfather dutifully went through the motions of picking Ronnie up and putting him in the floor of the car. I immediately began to cry.

He quickly asked me what was wrong, and I told him that he shouldn't have put Ronnie on the floor! He replied by telling me that dogs can't ride on the seat but must ride on the floor. I cried even harder and told him that Ronnie wasn't a *dog*—he was my *baby brother*! I'm so glad God blessed me with a loving and patient grandfather.

When I was four years old, my real baby brother was born. My parents had no choice but to name him Ronnie! I loved him from the bottom of my heart. The thoughts of anything happening to him could bring me to tears.

Pam and her "prayed for" brother, Ron.

The first day at the pool, I noticed a very tall, skinny kid about thirteen years old. I remember him looking like a skeleton with skin stretched over his bones. He was covered from head to toe with freckles. I just knew those freckles would wash off when he got in the water. He had bright orange hair and was badly sunburned. *That is some major ugly,* I thought to myself. *I don't want to get too close to him in case his freckles wash off of him and onto me!*

Mother and Carol Blake were sitting at an umbrella table close to the water's edge, talking to each other. Ronnie, who was four, was playing nearby in the wading pool. I was also playing in the wading pool but was quite a few feet from Ronnie. Suddenly, without warning, Ronnie lost his footing. Seconds later he was lying on the bottom of the pool and couldn't get up. I tried to call to my mother, but my screams stuck in my throat and nothing came out! I tried to hurry through the water to get to him, but my legs felt like lead! My precious baby brother was drowning, and I was completely helpless to save him!

Have you ever seen the television show where a character named Clark Kent steps into the telephone booth and miraculously changes into Superman? He would then take off with his red cape flying in the breeze to save the person in peril. Well, just like Superman, that tall, skinny, ugly kid came out of nowhere, jumped into the pool and quickly pulled my baby brother up from the bottom!

This boy instantly became much more than a skinny, ugly teenager. He was *Superman* in my eyes! He was suddenly transformed from the ugliest boy to the most beautiful angel I could ever imagine!

I'll never forget the look in my shocked and grateful mother's eyes as this young hero gently placed Ronnie in her lap, with my brother still sputtering and gasping for air. When she realized the magnitude of what could have happened, tears of joy ran down her cheeks.

I also remember how guilty I felt for the thoughts I had when I first laid eyes on this wonderful young man. Even though I was only a little girl, I knew that my judgment of him had been wrong, and I asked Jesus to forgive me.

Not only was I thankful that my brother's life was spared, but I was also grateful for a loving Savior who always looks on the inside. To God, we are all beautiful!

I love these words to a popular song, "Red and yellow, black and white, all are precious in His sight, Jesus loves the little children of the world!"

It is a lesson that has stayed with me all my life!

How is it with you, my friend? Do you feel that you are better than those around you? Has God blessed you with talent, looks, brains, money, or abilities that make you feel superior to your friends and neighbors? How about race or religious beliefs? Does your race make you feel superior? Do your religious beliefs tend to put people into neat little boxes and, if they don't fit, do you cast them aside? Ask God to show you your heart and to give you a love for those around you that you might think don't measure up! Remember, as sinful human beings, we look at the outward appearance but our perfect heavenly Father looks at the heart. Praise His holy name!

"Cat-Eyes" in the Sand

"And be sure your sin will find you out." Numbers 32:23, NKJV

"I can't find my glasses, Mrs. Singleton," I moaned to my teacher. "I've looked everywhere." When I was a little girl in the third grade, I began to have trouble seeing my schoolwork or my music when I practiced the piano. An eye test at the ophthalmologist revealed that I was far-sighted and needed glasses to do close-up work. I thought this was wonderful because I got to pick out some pretty frames. They were light pink and called "cat-eyes" because of their shape.

I couldn't wear them all of the time because they magnified everything; which meant that I had to carry them to and from school every day. This was before the days of backpacks, so my mother bought me a little purse to put them in so I wouldn't lose them. Being a bit of a tomboy, I soon got rid of the purse! It wasn't long before I lost the case to the glasses as well! I walked to school with my friends every day and, most of the time, I would carry my glasses in my pocket or balance them on top of my books! Naturally, I was always losing them.

We lived in Albuquerque, New Mexico, which was a city that was situated in a natural bowl at the base of the mountains. Because of the risk of flooding, *arroyos* were dug and were prevalent all over the city. Arroyos are large channels that can fill up quickly with water. An arroyo is no place for children to play. Besides the water danger, oftentimes huge caterpillar tractors would be at the bottom filling the arroyo bed with sand. Most of the time the arroyos were dry and kids loved to run down the steep bank through the soft sand and then run up the other side as fast as their legs would carry them. My mother made it abundantly clear that it didn't matter what the other kids did . . . I was to stay out of the arroyo!

Every day I walked to school, which was about a quarter of a mile from our home. On the way I passed a large arroyo and would watch wistfully as the other kids would take the shortcut running through the arroyo. I was to obey my mother's strict rule to walk on the bridge over the arroyo.

It was a beautiful spring morning, and I was making my way to school with two of my friends. When we reached the arroyo, it was full of kids running down the bank and then running up the other side to safety. Some of the children were sitting and playing in the sand, as if they didn't care at all if they were late to school! Oh, it looked like so much fun and there wasn't a cloud in the sky.

A voice in my head began to tell me that there was no danger, and besides, my mother would never know! The temptation was too great. I took a deep breath and ran as fast as I could down the side of the steep bank. My skirt blew in the wind and I felt like I was flying. Down, down, down I went until I hit the soft sand where I had to work to stay on my feet and keep up my momentum to get to the other side. Happy as a lark, I skipped the rest of the way to school feeling elated over what I had done.

Quickly I got to my classroom and took my seat before the bell rang. I began to look for my glasses and, much to my horror, they were nowhere to be found! What would I do? I couldn't see to do my homework without them!

Mrs. Singleton, who had the patience of the saints, said, "Pam, you'll just have to go to the office and call your mother to see if you left them at home." They were not to be found at home, so Mother drove to school, and together we walked the playground looking carefully for my little, pink, cat-eye shaped glasses.

Finally, my mother had an idea. "I know," she said. "Let's retrace your steps. We'll walk back the same way you came to school and maybe we'll find them." I was having so much fun on this little adventure that I didn't think about the trouble I was headed for!

"OK!" I said joyfully. We walked along the sidewalk holding hands and singing a little tune while we looked carefully for the glasses. Then suddenly, looming up before us like a gigantic pit, was the arroyo! *Oh no!* I thought to myself. *What am I going to do?*

All of a sudden, it was just as if a dark cloud covered the sun, the birds fell out of the trees, all of the flowers wilted, and my life of eight whole years passed before me! I suddenly remembered the text, "And be sure your sins will find you out." Mother began to walk toward the bridge that went over the arroyo, but I stopped. I felt sick to my stomach, but I had to tell her the truth.

"Mom, I didn't walk around the arroyo like you told me to. I went through the arroyo. I'm so sorry! I'll never do it again, I promise!" As long as I live I will never forget what I saw when I looked into her face. She looked so sad and very disappointed. And even worse, there were tears in her eyes! I determined that I would never do anything again to make my mother sad or disappointed in me. I loved her too much!

Without saying a word, she took my hand and we walked carefully down the steep bank of the arroyo. As our eyes scanned the surface of the sand, we saw something shiny. It actually hurt our eyes to look at it. Taking a closer look, we found them—my pretty pink glasses! They had been pushed down into the sand by a caterpillar tractor. We knew this because of the huge tire track that ran right over them. Only the corner of the glasses was sticking out of the sand and there was a small part of the lenses that was reflecting the sun.

I expected to find them busted to pieces, but there was not a scratch on them! The soft, deep sand had protected them. I believe that my guardian angel protected them as well. Needless to say, I learned a valuable lesson that day, and I never went through the arroyo again.

Friend, do you love the Lord? I mean, do you really love Him so much that the thought of disappointing Him makes you turn from your temptation and sin? I wish I could tell you that I never made any mistakes again, but you and I know that wouldn't be true. We are all sinners, but just as my mother did not disown me when I disobeyed, Christ doesn't cast me aside either. In contrast, look at the failures of Peter. The Bible reveals that Peter definitely sinned and even denied that he knew Jesus, but he came back to his Lord and repented. It doesn't matter how ugly our sin, Jesus is always ready to forgive, restore, and to give us power to overcome every temptation. Praise His holy name!

Stuck in the Mud

Purge me with hyssop, and I shall be clean;
wash me, and I shall be whiter than snow. Psalm 51:7, NKJV

"Watch, Mom, and notice how each rider keeps their engine at full throttle until they get to the other side of the mud puddle." What came next was great for a pig, but not for my mother!

Growing up, one of our favorite places to go on vacation was Red River, New Mexico. Red River, a tiny, rustic, western resort town, is nestled in the Rocky Mountain range in the northeastern part of the state. The whole area was, and still is, absolutely gorgeous. My mother rode the trails high in the mountains on horseback when she was a kid, so she knew the area like the back of her hand.

Pam on Sadie.

Mother had a good friend named Opal who lived in Red River. She owned horses that she would rent to the tourists. As soon as we arrived in Red River and got settled into our cabin, we would head to the stables to reserve our favorite horses for the next day. I always got Sadie. She was gentle and slow. Perfect for a little girl. Opal always gave Mother her personal horse because of Mom's riding ability. The name of her horse was Twist. Believe me, this was a perfect name for this horse! To mount her, the rider would have to turn the stirrup around so that the horse's head was to the rider's right. The rider would then place her boot in the stirrup and swing up and around to finally be mounted on the horse. If the rider tried to mount the horse in a normal manner, the horse would twist around and kick the person! Thus her name, Twist!

We were all way up in the mountains on a ride, and we had stopped to have our lunch. I remember sitting on a log, eating my sandwich and enjoying the incredible view. The fluffy white, billowy clouds were breathtakingly beautiful floating across the blue sky. Tall pine trees graced the green meadow with its clusters of wild flowers. There was a flock of sheep and their old shepherd on horseback. It all looked like a lovely painting.

Finally, Mom reminded us that we needed to get going before the rain moved in. It rained just about every afternoon in the mountains, and we tried to make it back to town before it started to come down. Without thinking, Mom attempted to mount Twist in the normal way. To everyone's horror, Twist kicked high and hard! She missed Mom's head by hairs and sent her cowboy hat sailing across the big, green meadow! With thankful hearts to Mother's guardian angel, we headed down the mountain.

Pam on her bike.

Years later, when my younger brother and I were well into our teens, we all traded the horses in for trail bikes—the kind with motors. About thirty of our friends from Texas would make the drive. They preferred to camp, so they all pitched their tents in a beautiful campground. We had a small Winnebago motorhome that we stayed in. No sleeping on the ground or using an outhouse. The Winnebago was about as close to camping as my mother would get!

We were so excited about the big ride. Some of the men rode some pretty tough and powerful bikes. They were looking forward to getting off the main trail where they could do some raw climbing. Some of the women rode on the backs of the bikes their husbands were riding. Some had their own bikes.

Mother and I each had a small Honda that was just like riding a little mountain goat. They were simple, sturdy little machines that were easy for us to operate. Or so I thought!

The morning of the big ride dawned bright and beautiful. I dressed quickly in jeans, a shirt, tennis shoes, and a lightweight jacket. My mother, however, came out in an "outfit." She wore royal blue jeans with a matching jacket. The whole outfit was stitched with a white topstitch. To finish things off, she wore little, white, vinyl boots! This was in style in the late sixties, but not appropriate for riding motorcycles in the mountains!

Mom—minus the mud!

Everyone got on their motorcycles, and we started out on the trail. I rode toward the back with Mom, as she was still learning how to ride her bike. We were having the best time, and everything was going well until we came upon the biggest, thickest, gooiest mud puddle I've ever seen. It covered the width of the trail, which was wide enough for a jeep to fit, and it was about ten feet long. There was no way around it. We had to go through it! My mother freaked. "I can't go through that!" she said. I told her she had plenty of power, and if she would just keep her throttle wide open and steady like everyone else was doing, she could make it. I sat with her on the side of the trail, and we watched until everyone had gone through without any trouble. Finally, we were the only ones left. Everyone had crossed and gone on their merry way.

I told Mom that I would go first. So, I gave it full power and away I went. The mud was so thick that my bike needed all the power I could give it. I got across without any problem. I looked back at Mom and said, "See, I did it. You can too. Just give it all the power you've got!" With a determined look, Mom started out, but not with full power. I knew she was in trouble. Sure enough, when she got to the middle of the mud puddle, her bike began to bog down in the mud until it came to a complete stop. The thought of putting her little white boots down in that mud to catch herself was more than she could handle. To my horror and amazement, I watched as she and her bike fell over into the mud! She looked as if someone drew a line down the middle of her! Half of her was still perfect and the other half was covered in mud! And then she began to laugh. She thought the whole thing was hysterical! When I realized she was not hurt, I had a good laugh too. One of the things I loved about my mother was her sense of humor. It didn't matter the situation, Mother would always see the humor in things. No one had seen her hit the mud but me, thankfully. So we turned around and rode back to camp to a nice, warm shower!

You know, it doesn't matter what kind of mud we're stuck in or how we got there. When we come to Jesus, He will wash us in His blood and cleanse us from all of our impurities. We don't have to do the washing or the cleansing. We don't have to change. We just have to repent and surrender. He will do the changing and the cleansing. What He did for us at the cross, our mortal minds cannot comprehend. But as the Bible says, "For whosoever shall call upon the name of the Lord shall be saved" (Romans 10:13, KJV). Won't you call on Him today?

Freddie

"I am the way, the truth, and the life. No one comes to the Father except through Me." John 14:6, NKJV

It was 1968, and I was eighteen years old. You can do the math! I was a senior at a very large public high school in Albuquerque, New Mexico. There were over six hundred students in my class alone. About 80 percent of the student body was Catholic and of Spanish descent. To my knowledge, I was the only Seventh-day Adventist Christian in the school.

I had many friends, and I participated in as many school activities as possible without compromising my beliefs. For instance, someone would ask me if I was going to the football game on Friday night. I would tell them No and explain to them that it was the Sabbath, God's holy day. They would reply by telling me to "just go ask my priest." I informed them that my Priest already said No! I was teased a lot in a friendly sort of way, and they seemed to respect me even though they didn't completely understand.

One of my closest and dearest friends in junior high and high school was Freddie Herrera. We never dated, but were always good friends. Freddie was a Catholic, and although his mother made him go to Mass and confession, it didn't hold much meaning for him. I don't think he ever completely bought into the idea that he had to confess his sins to another human in order to be forgiven. Nevertheless, he thought my religion was *really* strange, and he did his fair share of teasing.

Freddie struggled in school but he excelled in athletics. He was extremely gifted and lettered in every sport the school offered. It didn't matter if it was football, baseball, basketball, track and field, or anything else. Whatever the sport, Freddie excelled.

One hot Friday afternoon in May, Freddie and his friend Oscar came over to my house with the idea in mind that I was going to learn to play basketball and they were going to teach me. Believe me, it was going to be a chore for everyone involved! As I was running around the court frantically trying to get the ball *somewhere close* to the basket, I noticed that the sun was sinking lower and lower in the sky. Evangelist Kenneth Cox was holding meetings in Albuquerque and had asked me to sing that night. I didn't dare tell Freddie about the meetings. He didn't even know I could sing. The teasing over that fact would just be too much!

Realizing that I was running out of time, I was able to coax Freddie and Oscar into the house with the idea that Mother probably had some lemonade and cookies. As they sat at the kitchen bar inhaling their snack, I stood behind them and motioned to my mother by pointing to my watch. She knew exactly my predicament. But with a smile and a twinkle in her eye, she asked them, "How would you boys like to come and hear Pam sing tonight?"

They turned to look at me and with big grins said, "Pam sing? We wouldn't miss it!"

I was furious with my mother, to say the least!

Mother told them what time to be ready, and as we drove to pick them up, I thought, *These guys attend a huge, beautiful Catholic cathedral and we are taking them to a big, brown tent that has sawdust on the ground, white backless benches, and pictures of some of the most horrific looking beasts a person could ever imagine!* I was sure my mother had ruined my life!

I can't remember what I sang that night, but I remember Kenneth's sermon was on the mark of the beast! As he preached, the boys' eyes got bigger and bigger. They were learning things from the Bible they had never, ever heard before. However, Kenneth also preached about a loving God who invites us to come and have a personal relationship with Him. They had never heard that before either.

On the drive home, they had a million questions for Mother! She gave them each a Bible and some other books that she thought might help.

I don't remember much after that. We graduated in June, and Freddie joined the army. The Vietnam War was going on strong, and many of our friends were coming home in flag-draped caskets. I begged Freddie not to join. With his athletic ability, he could get a full scholarship to any college of his choice. Once accepted, the likelihood of him being drafted was small. He told me he wasn't smart enough to go to college and his mind was made up.

Freddie joined the army and went straight to boot camp. Soon after that he was on his way to Vietnam. He wrote at first, but then the letters stopped coming. We soon learned that he had been captured along with his whole platoon and was a prisoner of war. I never saw Freddie again.

When the American forces arrived at the camp where Freddie and his platoon had been imprisoned, they began to gather the soldier's personal belongings. Can you guess what they found of Freddie's? His Bible!

I am so thankful that my mother listened to the Holy Spirit as He prompted her to invite my friends to Kenneth's meeting on that Friday night. I feel certain that Freddie had given his heart to Christ and had learned that Jesus was just a whisper away during any trial or torture he had to endure. And I also believe that I will see my dear friend again when Jesus comes in all of His glory and majesty to take us home. Will you be there too?

The Devil's Trap

Jesus rebuked the demon, "Stop shouting and come out of him!" Immediately the demon threw the man down and into convulsions and then with a shriek, left him. Mark 1:25, 26, The Clear Word

Back in the early seventies, my husband, Jimmy, visited the country of Ethiopia with Mission Spotlight. Early one Sabbath morning, he and his group traveled by foot into the jungle for a baptismal service. His job was to record the event for a Mission Spotlight story to be shown in Seventh-day Adventist churches in North America. During their walk to the river, the interpreter shared with them that sometimes the devil would interfere with the baptism by exposing his anger through some of the baptismal candidates. Upon hearing this, Jimmy prayed for the Lord's protection and an extra outpouring of the Holy Spirit.

After they reached the river, Jimmy set up his recording equipment and dangled the microphone from a tree branch that hung over the baptismal area. A few minutes into the service, a young lady was led into the water. When she got about knee-deep into the river, she suddenly began jumping and screaming. She ran out of the water and fell flat on her back on the shore. She was foaming at the mouth and bouncing her head against the ground. Terrible sounds were coming from her mouth. She began to choke and became very hysterical.

Her body started levitating off the ground, and a few of the native ministers tried to hold her down. Church members began praying. One of the ministers began to read from the Bible where Jesus rebuked the demon. As soon as he said, "By the power in the name of Jesus, I command you to come out of her," she became calm and still. She was then led back into the water and was baptized.

Jimmy recorded the service on tape. The words and sounds out of this young lady's mouth were from the devil. This was verified when the tape was reviewed and the interpretation was, "Leave her alone! She's mine and she is not to be baptized."

Here in America, the devil sometimes performs in more subtle and sophisticated ways. He works through the media, television, movies, video games, and the printed word. Spiritualism is everywhere. Books designed for children are full of spiritualism, and many parents and teachers think the magic and spiritualism portrayed in these books are just harmless creativity. They take the position that as long as the kids are reading, it doesn't matter what they read. But they are wrong and are making a huge mistake. Children's minds need to be carefully guarded and protected from the enemy. If only parents and teachers could be transported back to Ethiopia and witness the evil power in its raw form!

The Bible tells us in Deuteronomy 18:11, 12 that being "a medium or a spiritist, or one who calls up the dead," is an "abomination to the LORD" (NKJV). Satan doesn't care how he does it, or what means he uses to separate us from Jesus! He just wants to win, whatever it takes! He will leave no stone unturned in order to watch us fall. He uses many attractive avenues to lure us away from Jesus.

Television is one of his favorite tools. It's hard to find good, clean, uplifting programs anymore unless you are watching a Christian channel. Many programs feature attractive people who talk with the dead. In fact, it is hard to find a current television program that doesn't glorify the devil. Adults and kids alike are fascinated with the occult world, magic, werewolves, vampires, and all kinds of witchcraft, all cleverly designed to take us down the path of sin.

The devil knows his time is short. He will stop at nothing to invade our minds and ruin our lives. Our only safety is spending time every day in prayer and in the study of God's Word. We must train our children while they are still young to do the same. When we leave the Lord out of our daily routine, the devil takes over. He doesn't ask; he just simply steps in. So much for the idea that we control our own lives!

I'm so glad we have an awesome God who conquered the devil and all of his wickedness. We know the end of the story! We know who wins the battle between good and evil! We have nothing to fear. We only need to surrender our hearts to God. Recommitting our lives to Jesus every day is our best and only protection from Satan and his devious, wicked ways. When you are tempted by worldly pleasure, say out loud, "Jesus, save me!" He stands ready to send tens of thousands of angels to be by your side! At the mere mention of the name of Jesus, the devil will flee! Praise God!

Before You Call

"It shall come to pass that before they call, I will answer; and while they are still speaking, I will hear." Isaiah 65:24, NKJV

"What are we going to do?" The conference president moaned to himself. "There is just not enough money in the bank. We are in need of a major miracle!"

In 1972, the headquarters of the Texaco Conference of Seventh-day Adventists was located in Amarillo, Texas. The territory of this conference included the panhandle of Texas and the state of New Mexico. Currently, the state of New Mexico is the fourth poorest state in the U.S. Back in the sixties and seventies, I'm sure it was even worse. Anyone working for the church in New Mexico at that time could consider himself a missionary. But to me it was home. The church people were warm and loving. I have many wonderful memories of growing up in the Albuquerque church.

Lota Burger, 1952.

My dad was a businessman in Albuquerque. He sold hamburgers out of little "drive-in" restaurants, as they were called back then, and he was expanding by leaps and bounds throughout the state. My parents started the business in 1952, and, before long, they were hugely successful. My father was a generous man and believed in God. Although he was not a Seventh-day Adventist, Dad faithfully paid his tithes and offerings to the local Adventist church where we attended. The more he gave, the more God blessed him. He grew up in a Baptist home, and he said his dad taught him to always pay tithe. I heard my dad say many times that you couldn't *out-give* the Lord!

One example was when the conference president called all his employees into the boardroom. "This is serious, folks! We need to pray such as we have never prayed before! We are in a financial crisis! We've written many checks, but there just isn't sufficient funds to cover them. We must plead with the Lord to help us and to help us ASAP!"

His secretary returned to her desk and began to pray. A few minutes later, she was interrupted when the mail was delivered. There, right on top of the stack, was a letter from my dad. Quickly, she picked it up and quietly scurried into the boardroom. "I think you might want to open this," she whispered into the president's ear. "It's from Blake Chanslor."

Lota Burger today.

With trembling hands, the president opened the envelope. Inside he found a check from my dad. It was made out to the Texaco Conference and the amount was more than generous! It was enough to cover all the checks they had written . . . with some left over!

Believe me, there was some serious rejoicing in the boardroom that day! Everyone was reminded that even before they prayed, God was sending help. God loves each one of us and He knows just what we need. This was just another one of God's miraculous answers to prayer and an affirmation that our God will supply all our needs!

How is it with you, my friend? Are you trusting God with your tithes and offerings even when you can't afford it? If you are, then no matter how large or small the gift, God will bless you. Remember, you can't out-give the Lord!

Are you trusting God with your life or are you carrying the weight of the world on your shoulders? I invite you today, this minute, to turn everything over to Him. I love the old hymn, "God Will Take Care of You."

> *God will take care of you,*
> *Through every day, o'er all the way;*
> *He will take care of you,*
> *God will take care of you.*

We are not promised that this life will be easy, but God does promise to be with us in times of trouble. If we commit to Him, He will take care of us . . . even before we ask!

"You're Fired!"

Trust in the LORD *with all your heart,*
and lean not on your own understanding; in all your ways acknowledge Him,
and He shall direct your paths. Proverbs 3:5, 6, NKJV

It was my seventh birthday and I'll never forget seeing my dad get out of his company truck with a white sack from the drugstore. I met him on the porch and, with a big grin, he bent down and handed me the sack.

"Happy birthday, honey," he said.

I carefully opened the sack and took out the largest box of crayons I'd ever seen!

He knew Mother had gotten me something special from both of them, but he wanted to buy something that would be just from him!

Pam and her daddy.

Growing up, my dad was always a source of encouragement for me. When I was thirty and thinking of getting braces on my teeth, he told me to go ahead.

"I don't want you to have ugly teeth like mine," he said sadly.

When I was toying with the idea of getting a master's degree, but dreading the six long summers and all the hard work, he said that the six summers were going to pass anyway, so why not get the master's? It was Dad that suggested I might try business school when I wasn't sure about college and what I wanted to do with my life. With those skills, I could surely get a job anywhere. That was one encouragement he lived to regret!

I enrolled in a local business college, and I quickly realized I was a square peg in a round hole! I was bored silly! Not because it was all easy, but because it wasn't the right fit for me. I didn't have the aptitude for it. I didn't want to disappoint my dad, so I gritted my teeth and plowed through it!

In the meantime, I applied to La Sierra College and was accepted for the second semester. I was so excited! I was looking forward to living on a beautiful campus and enjoying the Adventist Christian atmosphere. Having always attended public schools, which were very nice and gave me a great education, the opportunity of being with people who believed like I did was very appealing.

I had a couple of months before I was scheduled to leave for La Sierra and I needed to find a job. But who was going to give me a job for just a couple of months?

"Why don't you come down to my office and work with my accountants?" my dad suggested. "They're working on taxes, and I'm sure they could use the help."

"Oh thanks, Dad," I responded, trying to look grateful. But on the inside I was screaming, *Someone deliver me, please!* After thinking about it a while, I decided I should take Dad up on his offer. *After all, I can do anything for a short time,* or so I thought!

Soon the first day of work came. I thought to myself, *No one is going to want to work with the boss' daughter. They're going to hate this as much as I will.*

But much to my delight, they were all friendly and welcoming. They showed me to my desk and gave me my first task. As soon as I finished, there was something else to take its place. I thought the day would never end!

This is so boring! I thought. Trying to spice up the day, I began to chat with all the staff. It wasn't too long before I had them laughing their heads off!

Now this is just what this place needs. A little fun! I thought, smiling to myself. All of a sudden, from the direction of my Dad's office, came a big booming voice.

"PAM, GET IN HERE!"

Quickly everyone buried their heads in their work, and it was so quiet that I'm sure you could hear a pin drop! I scurried down the hall to Dad's office.

Pam and her dad.

Upon entering I acted innocent and said, "Yes, Daddy?"

"You're fired! Go home!" he announced firmly.

"But Daddy, I need the money!" I pleaded.

"I'll pay you, but just go home!"

I thought to myself, *Wow, that's not a bad deal!* So I quickly said, "OK, Daddy!" And that was the end of my office career.

How about you? Are you stuck in a job or career that makes you miserable? Just because my dad was a successful businessman and enjoyed the business life didn't mean that I was cut out for the same thing, even though I was his daughter! Luckily he didn't try to force me to be what he wanted me to be, like so many parents do. He knew my talents lay elsewhere.

Some people's talents are obvious, like my husband, Jimmy, for example. He can play just about any instrument his hands touch! At the age of seven, he was playing for every event in his little country church. He believes anyone can play like he does if only they would practice! But I'm not so sure! I took piano lessons for seven years and practiced faithfully . . . and I can't play a note!

We have a heavenly Father who has a plan for each of us, if we would only ask and believe. A text in the Bible, which holds a special place in my heart, is found in Proverbs 3:5, 6, "Trust in the LORD with all your heart, and lean not on your own understanding; in all your ways acknowledge Him, and He shall direct your paths."

God wants you to know that you are unique and that He has given you special talents and abilities. He will direct your paths and show you what to do. God is faithful and has proven this text over and over in my life. He'll do it for you too. He may ask you to do something for Him, but you think you don't have the talent. God will provide everything you need to do the job. We just need to trust Him!

The Hot Iron

Be anxious for nothing, but in everything by prayer and supplication, with thanksgiving, let your requests be made known to God; and the peace of God, which surpasses all understanding, will guard your hearts and minds through Christ Jesus. Philippians 4:6, 7, NKJV

Steam came out of the iron as I began to iron my husband's shirt. I felt as if steam was coming out of my ears as well! We had recently moved from Pasadena, California, to the tiny town of Cleveland, Tennessee. I had been excited about the move because we could raise our children in a more rural environment, and Jim's new job would offer him many wonderful opportunities. What I hadn't bargained for was the amount of time he would be gone from the kids and me. I was lonely, frustrated, and totally immersed in self-pity!

On the floor of our tiny apartment sat our beautiful, ten-month-old, baby daughter, Rondi, playing happily with her toys. With one eye on her, I continued ironing—and feeling sorry for myself. I began to pray, telling God all of my troubles. *Have You left me, Lord? Did Jimmy and I run ahead of You when we decided to make this move? Do You still love me?*

Suddenly, I heard the most awful blood-curdling scream! It came from an upstairs bedroom where our three-year-old son, Jimmy, was playing. Without thinking, I rushed up the stairs to see what had happened. He had jumped off of something and had landed on the side of his foot. I scooped him up into my arms and began to comfort him. His foot seemed to be fine, but I told him I would get an ice pack just in case.

As I came down the stairs to get the ice pack, it hit me! *The baby! The hot iron! Oh no! How could I have been so careless?* With my heart racing, I rushed back into the room where I had left her. She greeted me with a big grin as she held up her new toy. It was the electrical cord to the iron! The iron, hot as a firecracker, lay just a few inches away!

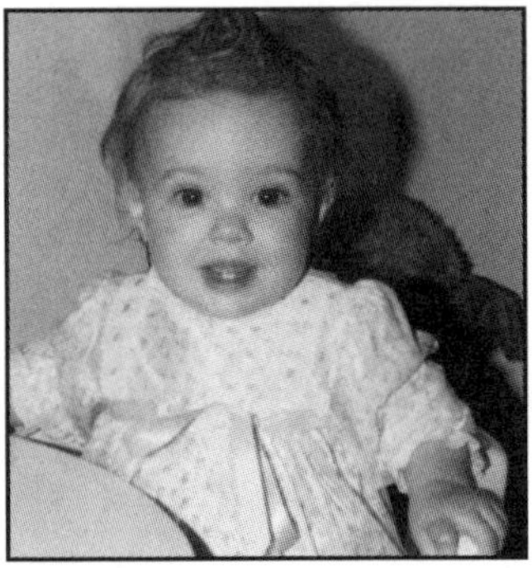
Rondi Rhodes, 10 months old.

Getting tired of her toys, she had decided to go exploring. She had crawled across the room, spotted the dangling cord, and pulled on it. The iron came crashing down, just missing her head!

With my baby girl in my arms, I sank to my knees with a prayer of thanksgiving for the angel He sent to protect my daughter. I told the Lord how sorry I was for doubting Him and how I knew for certain that He loved me. He did not need to send me any more reminders! His hot iron "message of love" came through loud and clear!

Rondi is now a young woman with children of her own, but every time I think of what could have happened to her, I get goose bumps! There is a beautiful song that I think of when I tell this story. It goes as follows:

Now I know He loves me, yes I know He loves me,
Life is so exciting since He came my way!

Just like Peter, I had taken my eyes off of Jesus and began to focus on the storm around me. Then I began to sink. But Jesus, in His love and mercy, reached out to me and pulled me up, releasing me from my selfishness and self-pity!

Dear friend, do you long to know that you are loved? Do you long to be freed from the sins that so easily beset you? Put your eyes upon the Master. Spend time with Him everyday, getting to know Him and His character. He longs to love you, forgive you, set you free from your sins, and finally save you for His kingdom! How awesome is that?

Bobby's Miracle

Now to Him who is able to do exceedingly abundantly above all that we ask or think, according to the power that works in us, to Him be glory in the church by Christ Jesus to all generations, forever and ever. Amen. Ephesians 3:20, 21, NKJV

I was privileged to teach first and second grade in our Adventist school in Cleveland, Tennessee, for eleven years. If the truth were known, in all the years I spent teaching, God taught me more through those children than I ever taught them.

Case in point—Bobby.* It was a busy, but organized, first day of school in my classroom. Parents were helping their children get settled when . . . in came Bobby. He was the cutest little fellow and actually appeared shy as he hid behind his mother. However, as we all know, looks can be deceiving. Actually, he was every teacher's worst nightmare! He could not sit still. He could not keep his hands to himself. He could not concentrate. He talked all of the time. And the saddest thing was that the other children would not have anything to do with him. I thought to myself, *Now I'm a master teacher. I'll have this child straightened out in no time!*

I began to use one behavioral theory after another trying to tame this little boy. Instead of getting better, he got worse! I suspected he had attention deficit hyperactivity disorder, better known as ADHD. I said to myself, *I will recommend that he be tested, the doctor will give him some medication, and life will be rosy once again!* Wrong! He didn't have ADHD, and by this time I needed the medication!

One day the Lord spoke to my heart. *"Pam, you haven't given Bobby to Me. Why are you trying to fix him without Me?"* It was like I had been struck with a thunderbolt! How could I call myself a Christian teacher? I had left the Lord out of the whole process! I immediately repented and said, "Lord, Bobby is all Yours!"

When I went to school the next morning, Bobby came bouncing in early as usual. I said to him, "Bobby, would you like to pray with me, just the two of us?"

"Oh yes, Mrs. Rhodes. That would be cool."

We found a quiet spot and began to pray. We prayed for Bobby, and we prayed for Bobby's teacher. Change didn't happen in a matter of weeks, or months. No, the miraculous thing was that I actually began to see a change in Bobby that very day! And the change continued the next day and the next!

Every morning Bobby and I would have prayer together. Day by day, Bobby's bad habits began to improve. He was doing beautifully in all of his subjects and the children were beginning to enjoy him. The faculty noticed the difference and asked if Bobby had been put on medication. I told them No, but I had called on the heavenly Pharmacist, and He had the perfect prescription! If for some reason I would forget our prayer time, Bobby would come up to me, tug on my clothes, and say, "Mrs. Rhodes, we haven't prayed yet."

One day Bobby's mother came in to see me after school and asked, "Are you praying with my son?"

I looked into her eyes and responded, "Yes, I am!"

Tears began to trickle down her cheeks. She said, "Bobby came home and asked if we could pray together like he did at school with his teacher. He asked if we could go back to church like we used to. My son told me, 'Jesus is my "bestest" Friend! He is helping me to be a good boy.' " She continued, "Because of you, our family is back in church!"

I thanked her, but told her that none of this incredible and wonderful miracle was of my doing! If I had gone about things *my way,* I would still be trying to fix him with my educational techniques!

---

* *Bobby is not the actual name of the student.*

We have a marvelous and all-powerful God that is longing to help us with every problem. There is no problem so big He cannot solve it. There is no mountain so big He cannot move it. There is no storm so dark He cannot calm it, and there is no sorrow so deep He cannot soothe it. For He carried the weight of this old sinful world upon His shoulders, and I know, my friend, that regardless of what you are dealing with, He can carry you!

Son of Nun

The Lord *spoke to Joshua the son of Nun. Joshua 1:1, NKJV*

"Please, *pleeeease* Mrs. Rhodes, can I be a team captain?" I would hear this plea from one of my first- or second-grade students every time we played the game Egypt to Canaan.

To play the game, two captains were chosen by the class, and then they would choose their teams. The team captains were the ones who moved the icons around the board. Each student was asked a question, in turn, from the Old Testament. If their answer was correct, then the team captain could move their icon the number of spaces indicated on the question card. The first team to reach the end won the game.

I had a first-grade boy who especially loved to play Egypt to Canaan. But little Ethan* struggled to remember the answers to the Old Testament questions. He also struggled with his schoolwork. He was actually very bright, but he didn't learn everything the same way the other kids did. He was actually a tactile learner. For example, he learned his spelling words better by writing them with his finger in something gritty like salt or sand than by writing them with pencil on paper. His brain seemed to receive and retain the information more clearly if he could feel what he was trying to learn. As his teacher, I was challenged, to say the least!

To prepare the children to play the game, at the beginning of the school year, I would read through some of the cards that asked them the Old Testament questions and made sure they knew the answers. We would take on a few cards at a time until we finally covered the whole stack. They were then ready to start playing the game.

Poor Ethan! He worked harder than anyone else to learn the answers to the questions. At times some of the other children would help him by drilling him.

Sometimes he would practice writing the answers in his saltbox. Whatever it took for him to be prepared to play the game, he was willing to do.

One day I announced to the class that I felt they were ready to play Egypt to Canaan. The children chose the two captains and then the captains chose who they wanted to be on their teams. Now, if these captains were picking kids to play ball, Ethan would have been picked first! He was very gifted at sports. But, because they were choosing students who were good at remembering the answers, in this game, Ethan was usually chosen last.

The children sat in a line on the floor with their team so that the two lines faced each other. The team captains sat first in their line with the game board between them.

I would then read the question card to each player. If they knew the answer, then their team captain moved the icon a number of spaces. If the student missed the answer, then the other team got the same question. We followed this pattern until everyone had a chance to answer a question.

So far the teams were doing very well. In fact, they were tied. Then it was Ethan's turn. Now, I must tell you that the children loved Ethan, but Ethan's team held their breath when they realized that Ethan was going to win or lose the game for them. In fact, I was holding my breath as well! I pulled out the next card and began to read the question.

"Who was the son of Nun?" Most of the children knew the answer and quickly slapped their hands over their mouths to keep from blurting out the answer or any clues! I reminded Ethan's team that they were not permitted to help him.

Little Ethan sat there, banging his fist against the side of his head and repeating over and over the question, "Who was the 'son of Nun'?" Finally, out of sheer desperation, he looked at me and said, "I don't know! Was it zero?"

I couldn't believe my ears. The correct answer, of course, was Joshua. But Ethan's answer, though incorrect, was hysterical and rather brilliant, to say the least!

I quickly excused myself and exited to the hallway where I burst into laughter!

Oh, how I loved that little boy! And, oh, how Jesus loved him more than I ever could! I'm so thankful that the Lord loves all of us even when we don't have the right answers. As a teacher, I believe that studying so that we are educated and well-informed is a worthy pursuit—especially when it comes to the Bible.

When I was a student at La Sierra College, in Riverside, California, I remember our campus chaplain, Elder Morris Venden, saying over and over, "It's not *what* you know that will save you. It's *who* you know."

---

* *Ethan is not the actual name of the student.*

Dear friend, do you know our Lord and Savior? Do you spend time with Him each day? You may not have all the answers to life's problems . . . but Jesus does!

Glasses in My Pocket

Be still, and know that I am God. Psalm 46:10, NKJV

It had been a hectic, busy day in my first- and second-grade classroom. School was dismissed and the children had all scampered away, but there was no end of the day for me as I looked at the piles and piles of papers that littered my desk. The classroom looked as if a bomb had gone off, and I had a headache to match!

As I slowly moved around the room picking up papers, pencils, toys, and books, and generally trying to put the room in order, I began to talk at God. Did you notice I said "at God" rather than "to God"? My mind was about as far away from Him as it could possibly be. I was muttering about all the paperwork I had to do before I could go home, and I couldn't find my glasses anywhere! *How in the world can I focus with my far-sighted condition and a headache to boot?*

I had always heard growing up that we are to talk to God as we would talk to a friend. I knew this to be true, as I would send messages up to my Lord as I went about my day. Sometimes they would be little prayers of thanksgiving. There were times when I would need immediate help with a student or a parent. Sometimes I would hear an ambulance off in the distance when out on the playground with the children. I would quickly send up a prayer for whoever might be injured. But this day was different. I was tired, hurting, and treating God like He was some kind of cosmic pet that I could totally ignore while asking for His help.

While I was treating Him with total disrespect, muttering, and attempting to find my glasses, He answered my prayer! He said to me, *"Kneel."* That stopped me in my tracks!

"Did You say for me to kneel?" I asked incredulously.

He repeated, *"Kneel."*

I quickly fled to a quiet spot, closed the door, and sank to my knees.

"Oh Lord," I prayed. "I'm so sorry for my disrespect. Please forgive me for treating You so commonly. You are my God and I love You. But, Father, I need my glasses." Suddenly, in my mind, I could see that my glasses were in my pocket. I carefully slipped my hand into my pocket and, much to my amazement, there they were!

At first I felt really foolish. That's right up there with wearing your glasses on top of your head while you frantically look for them. Or wearing them on your nose while you frantically look for them! Did I mention that teaching is stressful?

My sweet Lord knew exactly where those glasses were. He wanted to show me, but He wanted to do even more. When I felt those glasses in my pocket, I felt this huge relief. It was as if this heavy load lifted from my shoulders. My headache was gone as well, and suddenly I had renewed strength for all the many tasks ahead. When I focused on my Father, when I stopped moving and complaining, He was able to say, *"Be still, and know that I am God."*

What a powerful and mighty God He is. Friend, He doesn't just want to help you find your "glasses." He wants you to stop, sit quietly at His feet, focus on Him, and allow Him to help you. He will heal you and lift your heavy burden. He will do this as only God can, in His perfect timing and in His perfect way!

Over the Limit

God is our refuge and strength, a very present help in trouble. Therefore we will not fear, even though the earth be removed, and though the mountains be carried into the midst of the sea. Psalm 46:1, 2, NKJV

If there was anyone I was impressed to pray for, it was my brother Ron. From the time he broke his leg at age three to the time I saw him become airborne on his motorcycle, flying over a dirt mound! He survived a horrible car accident, a kidnapping, and he raced down every dangerous ski trail he could find. There was one named "Suicide" that went straight down at an angle no one could recover from if they fell, and he flew over it as fast as he could propel himself!

But the time I really prayed for him was the time he played the piano to accompany me to sing for church! He was a loving son and endured years of piano lessons to please our mother. No one knew that he could play, and the congregation didn't hear a note I sang because they were looking at him in total disbelief!

Dad and Ron with his broken leg.

When Ron was little, our father got a pilot's license. Dad bought a small plane that was loud and noisy. It scared Ron so much that he wouldn't get in it. It was hard to believe that there was actually something he was afraid of! However, that didn't last long. When he became old enough, he obtained his pilot's license as well, and he was a marvelous pilot. I felt safe enough to willingly fly anywhere with him!

Helicopters soon became his passion, and he signed up for lessons. He had ten helicopter hours when he began his search for a specific model helicopter. He went online looking for a 1968 Bell 47, turbo charged. He found one in Massachusetts that had been used to lift cranberries out of a bog.

The Bell helicopter.

He contacted the owner and made a trip to Massachusetts to buy the Bell 47. A man by the name of Herb Howe, an instructor, was hired to fly with Ron from Massachusetts to Albuquerque, New Mexico. Quite a trip to say the least!

The first leg of the trip was 230 miles to the Catskills in New York. They didn't quite make it as far as they planned, which meant they had farther to go the second day.

Up early the second day, they were preparing to take off when Ron began to fill the tanks on the fuselage. What he didn't know was the gas gauge read full when it was actually two gallons short! After a two-hour flight, they had a fourth of a tank and still had an hour to go! The gauge started bouncing on empty and they still had thirty minutes to fly! It stayed on empty, and they had no place to land. And if that wasn't enough drama, they were over forests in Pennsylvania—not a clearing anywhere to set the helicopter down!

Ron and his wife, Laura.

Herb began to tell Ron how he

would crash-land the plane, which was something Ron definitely did not want to hear! Herb's plan was to rotate down to the trees and fall through them backward! Ron uttered a quick prayer, "Lord, I'll see You in a minute!"

Then all of a sudden, they saw an airport at the edge of the trees! They were in total disbelief! It didn't take them too long to bring their thirsty, little bird to safety. They landed with a tank that holds sixty gallons and fifty-seven and a half of those are what is called "usable fuel." It took fifty-eight gallons! If you survive, that is one way to get old fast!

The devil is out to steal, kill, and destroy all of us any way he can. But Jesus has come that we may have life and have it more abundantly. He wants us to accept His offer of salvation, which is ours for the asking. He wants us to fuel up on His Word and lean on His power and grace. He wants us to share with others what He has done for us and about the home He's gone to prepare. And just as I've always prayed for Ron, He wants us to pray fervently for one another.

My friend, the devil knows his time is short. This old sin-sick world can't go on much longer. We're experiencing natural disasters like we've never seen before. Our world's economy is in serious trouble. Anything goes when it comes to our nation's morals. We are running out of fuel and falling fast. In these scary times, we must be reminded, "God is our refuge and strength, a very present help in trouble. Therefore we will not fear, even though the earth be removed, and though the mountains be carried into the midst of the sea" (Psalm 46:1, 2, NKJV). Praise God!

Delivered

The LORD *will deliver him in time of trouble. . . .*
You will not deliver him to the will of his enemies. Psalm 41:1, 2, NKJV

As our plane made its final approach for landing, I could hear the landing gear rumble into place. When I looked out the window, to my dismay, I saw that the runway was in horrible disrepair. The airport itself looked like it had been bombed! The grounds were unkempt, and there were weeds everywhere. Suddenly, I wasn't so sure about being a missionary. But, ready or not, Jimmy and I were landing near Zaporizhzhya, Ukraine, to help evangelist John Carter and his team reach precious souls with the good news of the gospel.

In the country of Ukraine, the government is supposed to ensure a certain amount of freedom for its citizens. We soon learned that the country was actually run by the Cossacks. The Cossacks were warriors that dated back to ancient Russian history. Currently they are Nationalists of the Russian Orthodox faith, and they hate Americans. The Nationalists are very rich, while most of the population is extremely poor. For example, in the grocery store parking lots, one would see expensive BMWs and Mercedes-Benzes. Only the rich could afford to buy their groceries at the grocery store.

The citizens scratch out a living the best way they can. Little grandmothers sell flowers on the street corners. Beautiful young women devote themselves to prostitution because they're sure to have a roof over their heads and plenty of food to eat. Highly trained physicians make only twenty dollars a month! Imagine a doctor studying for years in medical school, only to make twenty dollars a month! The cost of living at the time of our trip was about the same or higher than in the U.S. Coming from the "land of the free and the home of the brave" and "the land flowing with milk and honey," the whole economic situation was deplorable.

The water for much of the country was supplied by the same river system where the Chernobyl reactor exploded. Therefore, the cancer rate among the population was extremely high, and the overall health and nutrition of the people were not good, to say the least.

The police could not be trusted. They were known to stop a vehicle, make a false charge, and accept money to drop the charge. They had the power to make a person's life utterly miserable. For example, a young Adventist pastor who was very sick was moving his young family from one city to another. They were traveling in a very large truck that contained their furniture and all their worldly possessions. It was late at night when Pastor Nesteruk was pulled over by the police. They ordered him to completely unload the truck. With no money to give them, he had no choice but to follow their orders. They all stood around and watched as this young man with a high fever struggled to unload furniture and boxes all by himself in the bitter cold. His wife stayed in the truck with their little ones, trying to keep warm. After the police had ransacked everything, they told the young pastor he could go. They left him alone, frozen and sick, to load everything back into the truck all by himself!

We had our first encounter with the police at the airport after we landed. We went to the area for baggage claim and, much to our amazement, all of our bags had made it! Along with our suitcases, Jimmy had checked several cases containing musical instruments. These the police quickly confiscated. We tried to explain why we needed them, but with the language barrier we got nowhere. Later, one of the local Adventist pastors made the two-hour round trip from Zaporizhzhya to the airport where he was able, with God's help, to retrieve the instruments without paying a bribe. Praise the Lord! We were so thankful!

Pastor John's wife, Beverly Carter, has a burden on her heart for the children in whatever country she and her husband are holding meetings. I'll never forget the orphanage we visited in Zaporizhzhya. This orphanage housed children, ages infant to four years of age. The lady physician, who conducted our tour, was young and attractive, that is . . . until she smiled. When she smiled, her teeth were brown and showed signs of decay, probably due to malnutrition. This was a common sight among most of the people.

In the orphanage, the healthy babies were separated from the sick ones. There was one baby in particular who especially captured our hearts. He was so happy and laughed easily. When they placed him in my arms, I felt how rough his clothes were against my skin. As I held him, I could hear and feel his little lungs rattle with each breath he took. And he was supposed to be one of the healthy babies! Other little ones had such blank stares as their caregivers barked orders at them. One little toddler had beautiful dark eyes, but she looked so sad. Her little face haunts me to this day.

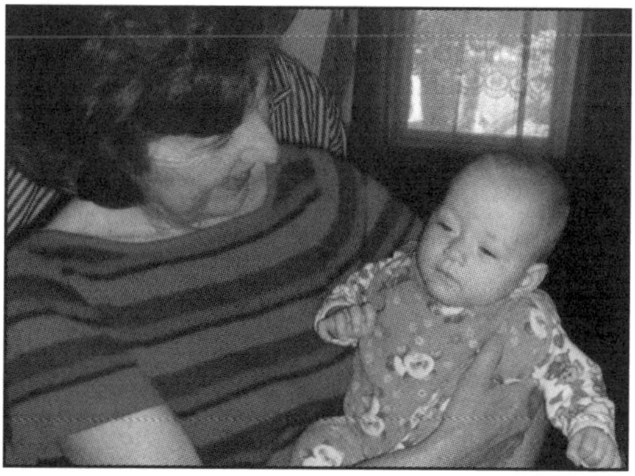

Beverly Carter holding one of the orphans.

The orphanage was in desperate need of a hot water system. The children's clothes were rough to the touch, in part because they were washed in cold, possibly radioactive, water and then dried on a clothesline. Beverly told the doctor that the Carter Report would supply the much needed hot water system. We all left feeling so helpless, wishing we could do more. That night I cried myself to sleep.

The meetings had been heavily advertised, and opening night was a huge success. There were so many people who were hungry to hear the message that Pastor Carter held two meetings each night! The auditorium was the best the city had to offer, but it was summer and the building had no air conditioning. With so many bodies packed into one place, it was very hot! With portable fans blowing directly on them, Pastor Carter and his translator, Vladim Butoff, preached passionately to an audience who had never heard the good news of Jesus.

The authorities knew who John Carter was and did their best to stop him. We soon learned that the government (the Cossacks) had announced on television that the meetings had been canceled. Pastor Carter promptly went to the television station, bought more time, and told the people that the meetings had not and would not be canceled. The Carter Report was always careful to stay within the law so that the government wouldn't have an excuse to legally shut the meetings down. Pastor Carter also had a security detail in place to protect him, Beverly, and anyone traveling with them.

The meeting hall.

To get to the meetings, the people would use their hard earned *hryvnias* to ride the buses to and from the auditorium. They would sacrifice food, if necessary, to be able to come to the meetings because they were desperate to learn more about Jesus. This precious Jesus, who died for them, was going to come back some day and rescue them from their poverty and hunger and give them a peace that passes all understanding.

Since the authorities had failed to cancel the meetings, they decided to stop the buses that serviced the auditorium. I'll never forget seeing the people coming from all directions. They were walking to get to the meeting, some of them for miles! Watching them, I wondered how Noah must have felt as he saw the animals coming to the ark. With Carter's tenacity and God's divine intervention, the buses were soon running the usual route in front of the auditorium.

I remember on the opening night of the meetings, I was so thrilled to see the people coming by the hundreds into the auditorium. I grabbed my camera to capture the happy faces of the people, both young and old. Suddenly, a lady came up to me and began talking very loudly. She pointed to my camera as she spoke. Finally, a light bulb clicked on in my head. "Oh, you want me to take your picture?" I asked. She plopped down in a nearby chair, folded her arms across her chest, and I took her picture! My friend, Nadija Nesteruk, who was one of our translators, came running up to me. Through her giggles, she told me that the lady was very angry that I was taking pictures of the people without their permission! And what was my response? I had taken *her* picture! The young people loved to have their pictures taken, but the older ones who grew up during Communism could not risk being photographed at a religious meeting!

Although I couldn't sing in Russian, the people seemed to be blessed by the music that Jimmy and I provided. All too soon it was time for us to go home. Packing our suitcases, we were careful to place a souvenir replica of a Cossack sword right on top of our clothes. We didn't want to appear to be hiding anything. We knew our grandson, who loved history, would be thrilled with the gift. At the time of our purchase, we were concerned that the airline wouldn't let us check it through. The merchant told us there would be no problem, but if they did question us, all we had to do was show them the receipt from his shop. We also checked with a couple of local pastors, and they told us the same thing. Just as long as the police knew it was a souvenir and not the real deal, there would be no problem.

There were two elderly ladies who had helped with the meetings that were also going home on our same flight. We got in line behind them and quickly realized that our checked luggage went through the X-ray machines in our presence. We were a bit nervous about them actually letting our "sword" go through. We watched as a bag went through that belonged to one of the ladies. It contained a large, sharp knife that she had used to prepare food in her hotel room. The second lady also had a sharp knife in her bag, but the officers let both bags go through without question. Then it was time for our bags. As soon as the X-ray picked up the sword, everything came to a standstill! Jimmy showed them the receipt from the souvenir shop, but it made no difference. They proceeded to pull us from line and put us in a small room. Also in the room were two very large officers and, thankfully, Pastor Volodia Nesteruk, who translated for us. Pastor Nesteruk began talking very fast, explaining that the sword was a souvenir for our grandson. He also told them who we were and why we had been in Ukraine. They didn't care. They took our passports and threatened to prosecute us!

One of the officers left the room along with our pastor. The other officer motioned for us to sit down. Jimmy and I were thinking the same thing. They probably want money! We weren't quite as elderly as the ladies and they probably thought a younger couple would be more able to offer a bribe. If this was the case, we were afraid to offer anything because then they could charge us with trying to bribe an officer. We couldn't win!

This whole ordeal went on for about forty-five minutes to an hour. Needless to say, we were praying the whole time. "Please Lord, get us out of this mess! And protect Pastor Nesteruk as well!" Suddenly, the officer and the pastor walked back into the room. We were handed our passports and told to go! They kept the sword, and we were so happy to be out of there that we didn't care!

As we thanked Pastor Nesteruk, he told us he was working to get himself and his family out of Ukraine and into the United States. I am happy to report that today, they are living in Spokane, Washington, where Volodia has a special ministry for the Russian people. God is so, so good!

We treasure our Ukraine experience more than we can express, and we were so amazed to see God perform one miracle after another on behalf of the Ukrainian people. We are so thankful that He performed a miracle on our behalf as well! Praise His holy name!

How about you, dear reader? Are you being held captive by an enemy of some kind? Maybe you have a bad temper or an addiction you can't kick. Whatever chains the devil has bound you with, the Savior can break them. He happens to be in the chain-breaking business! He loves you with an everlasting love and will deliver you from the devil's wicked control and give you peace. Won't you accept His deliverance and salvation today?

Runaway Wagon

The angel of the Lord *encamps all around those who fear Him, and delivers them. Psalm 34:7, NKJV*

"I'm so tired, Mama, can't we please go home?" cried little Mary Rhodes. Clutching Tilly, her baby doll, Mary sat on the wooden driver's seat at the front of the big wagon. My husband, Jimmy, who was ten at the time, along with their parents, were harvesting corn and throwing it in the back of the wagon just as fast as they could go. Harnessed to the wagon were the family's beloved horses, Blackie and Moonbeam. Blackie was as black as ink, and Moonbeam was a soft white, just like the moonlight that danced through Mary's bedroom window at night. Both horses were gentle by nature, and though they were *workhorses,* they were also family pets. My husband, Jimmy, remembers riding Moonbeam out to the mailbox every day to get the mail.

When they finished harvesting one section, Daddy Rhodes would take hold of the reigns of the horses, which hung off to the side for easy reach and, with a "yee-haw," move them farther down the row. Little Mary would hang on as the wagon bumped down the row. It was hard, backbreaking work, but the Rhodes were happy to have the farmhouse to live in and the job of working the big farm, even though someone else owned it. They were called "share croppers." The Rhodes family did the work, and, in return, they received 50 percent of the profits for their labor.

Daddy and Mother Rhodes believed in working hard and instilled their work ethic in their children. They also believed in God and taught their children that He was their Source for everything needed in this life. They taught Jimmy and Mary that Jesus was their Savior and He loved them so much that He was willing to die for their sins so that they could be in heaven with Him.

They began their day with morning worship, asking for God's protection as they headed for the fields to begin their work. They would end their day with evening worship, thanking Him for His blessings and His watch over them.

Mary and big brother Jimmy.

It was during worship and Bible study that Jimmy stated that he wanted to be a minister when he grew up. And he did. He became a minister of music in both his profession and in his outreach for the Lord.

Because Mary was too little to work, she would often ride in the wagon and play with her little doll, Tilly. It had been an unusually long day, and Mary was tired. She was ready to go home. Suddenly, without any warning, something spooked Blackie and Moonbeam. They took off with a bolt, running as hard as they could go across the field! However, they didn't stay in the plowed part, running in a straight line. No, instead they ran against the plowed furrows making it almost impossible for an adult to hang on, much less a child! Sitting up on the driver's seat, Mary was trying with all of her might to stay in the wagon. She began to scream for her daddy to stop the horses, but running as fast as he could, he could not catch the reins to bring Blackie and Moonbeam to a stop!

Out of the blue, for no apparent reason, the horses suddenly came to an abrupt halt! And miracle of all miracles, little Mary was still sitting in the driver's seat! Her daddy, in total disbelief, finally caught up to the wagon and took his daughter in his big, strong arms and comforted her.

That evening, the Rhodes family had a very special evening worship. They had no doubt that Mary's guardian angel had brought those horses to a stop and kept Mary in the wagon. As Jimmy and Mary look back at their childhood, they remember the verses their mother had them memorize. One of them was the verse chosen for this story: "The angel of the LORD encamps all around those who fear Him, and delivers them" (Psalm 34:7, NKJV).

Dear reader, I don't have to tell you about the dangerous world we live in. The devil knows his time is short, and he is seeking who he can kill and destroy, wherever he can. Do you take the time each day to consecrate your life and the lives of your loved ones to the Lord? Frankly, I don't leave home without Him. He's promised to send His angels with us for our protection. Sometimes tragedies happen anyway, but if we commit ourselves to Jesus, then no matter what, our lives are in His hands!

Oscar Performance

Be imitators of God, therefore, as dearly loved children and live a life of love, just as Christ loved us and gave himself up for us as a fragrant offering and sacrifice to God. Ephesians 5:1, 2, NIV

"Mom, I want to be a Pathfinder!" my nine-year-old son, Jimmy, announced. I instantly became sick to my stomach. "Why do you want to be a Pathfinder?" I asked.

"Because I could go camping and make things and, besides, my friends are joining!" he answered.

Camping? Surely he didn't mean *camping*!

As far as my husband and I were concerned, camping was as much fun as getting a root canal! But then I remembered that some of my happiest memories as a child were of being a Pathfinder and going to junior camp. I wanted Jimmy to have the same happy memories I did. However, I would never allow him to go camping unless my husband or I went too. Thus, the sick stomach!

I approached my husband, Jim, about the subject later that day. He had the same reaction. He agreed that Jimmy should have the outdoor experiences but he didn't want to go along anymore than I did.

"Why can't he go along without one of us?" he asked.

"Because he's only nine and I would worry!" I said.

"Then *you* should go!" my husband answered.

"He's not going to want his mommy tagging along!" I responded. "And besides, it would be an opportunity for you guys to do some special things together." I was saying this to a father who spent every spare moment he had with his children. He would come home from work and play with them, help with homework, read to them, and help them get ready for bed. But, the guilt trip worked.

Jimmy the Pathfinder.

"OK," he said. "I'll go!"

I reminded my husband that he would need to act really excited about going on the Pathfinder outings, so that Jimmy knew that his father was happy they were doing something special together.

Our son was overjoyed and Jim really threw himself into the whole experience. He trekked through the woods, carried a backpack, chopped wood, swam in the creek, cooked over an open fire, and looked for berries, special leaves, and bugs. He also took along a battery-operated keyboard and played while the kids sang songs around the campfire! Jimmy could have won an Oscar for his performance, and I thought he was having a grand time until he told me after returning from a camping trip that he felt he was being prepared for the "time of trouble"! But he loved his son more than anything, so he continued on.

One day while folding laundry, my son Jimmy came to me and said, "Mama, I've got a problem."

"What's the problem?" I asked.

"Well, I just don't know what to do!"

"To do about what?" I asked.

"Well, I don't think you're going to know what to do either because it's a pretty big problem!"

"Child, I can't help you if you don't tell me!" I answered impatiently.

"Well, I don't like Pathfinders anymore, but Dad is having so much fun that I don't know how to tell him that I don't want to go anymore. Should I just keep going so he won't be disappointed?"

Only by the grace of God was I able to keep myself from bursting into laughter! I looked into the sweet little face of my child. He was so sincerely concerned about depriving his dad of fun that he was willing to continue doing something that he no longer enjoyed. Like father, like son!

Normally, I would have insisted that my husband deal with the problem, but I wasn't sure if Jim could keep a straight face! I knelt down at eye level with my son and asked, "Honey, do you want me to take care of it for you? I think that I can handle it in such a way that Daddy won't feel bad."

"Really, Mom?" Jimmy sighed. "I would be so relieved!"

Not as relieved as your dad will be! I thought to myself as I watched my son scamper happily out of the room. I could hardly wait to tell Jim the good news, and I knew we would share a good laugh together!

What a precious husband God has blessed me with, who was willing to put his son's desires above his own! It made me love him even more!

Because our heavenly Father loves us so much and wants us to enjoy eternity with Him in heaven, He gave His life for us on Calvary. The Bible tells us that when we love one another, we are like a fragrant offering to God. It's easy to love God when we think of the ultimate sacrifice He made for us. But it isn't easy to love many of the unlovable people around us. Thankfully, God can cleanse our selfish hearts and give us the gift of loving and caring for our fellow man—even the difficult ones. It won't be a performance either. It will come as naturally as breathing in and out!

A Spoonful of Sugar

The contentions of a wife are a continual dripping. Proverbs 19:13, NKJV

It was a nightmare from which I just couldn't seem to awake! I was singing very loudly and totally off key. The audience didn't know whether to laugh or cry! Unfortunately, I wasn't dreaming. I was awake, and the whole thing was very, very real.

Let me start at the beginning.

Some years ago, Jimmy and I had been invited to provide music at the Illinois camp meeting. The Illinois Conference had purchased an electric piano from a dealer in Chattanooga and asked if we could bring it when we came. It was the exact piano that Jimmy played for our concerts, just a newer model. Using a computer disk that fit into the piano, Jimmy would layer sound on sound and then play *live* with what he had recorded. So, he checked our disks with the new model and everything worked perfectly. We picked up the new piano from the dealer, loaded it into our van, and we were off to camp meeting.

We were scheduled to give our concert Sabbath afternoon. Right after lunch, we began to set up the instruments and PA system. We then did a sound check, balancing my voice with the piano, organ, and tracks. Everything seemed to work just fine, or so we thought!

We were blessed with a large audience. People were so sweet to give up their Sabbath afternoon naps to come and hear us! As was our custom, we had prayer before we began, asking for the Lord's blessing on our program.

It was with confidence and faith in the Lord that I picked up the microphone and began to sing very softly. The song began to build in volume and with that, Jimmy began to let up on the soft pedal on the piano. Then something horrible happened. The piano shifted into a different key! Here I was holding this very loud note, using every ounce of breath I had, and my dear husband changed keys on me! The audience reacted with stunned looks on their faces! It was like they were all sucking on lemons!

I immediately stopped singing, and everything got very quiet. I looked at Jimmy and said, "Sweetheart, I can sing it in that key or I can sing it in the other key, but you've got to decide which one we're gonna do it in!" Jimmy grinned, got beet red, and the audience burst into laughter. We got through the rest of the concert without incident. Jimmy quickly realized that the piano, being new, had to be especially programmed not to do what it did—change keys when the soft pedal is released. Why? Who knows!

Everything turned out fine and the people enjoyed the whole incident as if it had been planned. But, unfortunately, it put me into a bad mood that I just couldn't snap out of. It was a very *long* trip from Illinois to Tennessee! Suddenly, Jimmy didn't seem to know *anything* about driving and he needed my help and advice with every turn of the wheel! I could hear myself nagging and nagging at him. He would just answer sweetly, "Yes, dear?" What a smart man I married!

I finally sent up a prayer to the Lord. "Father, please help me to stop nagging at my poor husband. It wasn't his fault the piano did what it did. Look at all the times he's covered for me when I messed up. Please Lord, close my mouth!" I said, "Amen," and then started right back up again!

It just so happened that it was our wedding anniversary. That fact didn't help things much! Coming into Nashville, Jimmy asked me if I wanted to stop at the Olive Garden restaurant for dinner to celebrate. I was in no mood for celebratory dinners, but quietly agreed.

We sat across from each other in a booth. He looked so handsome in the new sport shirt I had just gotten him. But what in the world was in his shirt pocket? *No, it can't be!* I thought to myself. It was! A great big plastic spoon perched big as life in his pocket! I couldn't believe it! It just set me off all over again. "Would you please tell me *why* you're walking around with a big plastic spoon stuck in your pocket?" With a twinkle in his baby blues, he said, "It's to catch all of the sugar that continually drips from your lips!" Now, was that inspired or what!

We both erupted into laughter and just about slid out of the booth on to the floor. Suddenly, the tension was gone. I fell in love with my husband all over again. After all these years, we still laugh about it. When I shared the story with my dad, he said, "You should buy the boy a shovel!" Thanks, Dad!

Does God have a sense of humor? You bet! I kept praying but seemingly got nowhere. Jimmy was praying too, and God, in His infinite wisdom, knew just what we both needed—laughter!

If you're a member of the human race and you enjoy relationships with your spouse, your children, parents, brothers, sisters, friends, church members and coworkers, and you don't plan on being translated any time soon, you're bound to have conflicts. Give those conflicts to the Lord and then stand back and watch Him work in creative and sometimes fun ways to resolve them! AND, ALWAYS keep a sense of humor! It's a gift from God—use it!

Standing on God's Promises

" 'Bring all the tithes into the storehouse, that there may be food in My house, and try Me now in this,' says the LORD of hosts, 'If I will not open for you the windows of heaven and pour out for you such blessing that there will not be room enough to receive it.' " Malachi 3:10, NKJV

"I don't know what I'm going to do," my friend lamented. "My business is almost down to nothing!" Charles* was the most gifted carpenter and craftsman I had ever met. His work was perfection and his ideas amazing. He had recently remodeled our kitchen and when he had finished, it looked like it could be featured on a magazine cover! The kitchen was so efficient with all of the latest bells and whistles that I was more than a bit intimidated when I attempted to make my first meal!

Charles and his wife were Christians and they knew that God had given him his talent. When work was scarce, he was tempted to find another job. But then everyone would remind him that he needed to stick with what God had designed him to do. Working with wood brought him happiness, and his finished products brought him joy when he knew he had captured just what the customer wanted—and then some! Unfortunately, in his profession, it was either feast or famine. When the economy went downhill, so did his workload.

As I listened to Charles talk about his lack of work, I quickly sent up a prayer asking God for wisdom. Then, seemingly out of the blue, I was impressed to ask him if he paid tithe. That kind of question seemed somewhat personal but God kept impressing me to talk to him about it. So I asked the question, telling Charles that he didn't need to give me the answer, but it was something to think about. I asked him if he would like me to type up some texts on tithing and drop them by. He was very receptive to the idea of tithing and wanted the texts.

Later that night, Satan began to whisper doubts into my mind. What if God didn't come through? What if His promise was not applicable to this situation? What if I was too much of a sinner for God to hear me? I flew to my knees and poured out my heart. "Lord, please come through for Charles. Show him that You are a loving God and that he can trust in Your promises."

I spoke with Charles the next day, and he told me that he had discussed the subject with his wife and she had agreed that they needed to pay tithe. Charles had just received an eight-hundred-dollar check—the last payment on a job. He quickly sat down at his desk and wrote out a tithe check. This was on a Friday, and he wouldn't turn in the check until Sunday. It wasn't long before his business phone rang. He had previously bid on a job, and his bid was accepted. The job for a sixteen-thousand-dollar kitchen was his! He got a call later in the day for another job! God was already working on Charles' behalf, even before the tithe check could be turned in!

Charles and his wife could hardly believe what had happened. God had been true to His promise. Charles told me later that he could hardly wait to pay tithe again just to see how a loving God would provide for His faithful children!

---

* *Not his real name.*

How about you, my friend? Are you faithfully fulfilling God's conditions? He longs to bless us and show us His love, if we would just take that first wobbly step toward Him. He will rush to scoop us up in His arms. He longs to show us that He is a God of love, a God of truth, and a God who is faithful to fulfill His promises!

Head Over Heels

God is our refuge and strength,
a very present help in trouble. Psalm 46:1, NKJV

"*Pray for Jimmy. Pray for Jimmy as he rides his bike.*" These words rang over and over in my head, seeming more and more urgent with time!

The Lord has richly blessed my husband and me with three beautiful kids. They are all adults now with homes of their own. If you are a parent, then you know that your love and concern for your children never goes away just because they have reached adulthood. It just changes with time and circumstances.

Our son Jimmy had become quite proficient at riding his racing bike. He was fast, and he especially excelled at powering up steep climbs. I knew he rode once a week with a group of friends and usually once a week with our son-in-law. I always prayed for his safety, as well as the safety of those with whom he rode. However, this time was different. The Lord had been impressing me, every day for the past week, to pray for him as he went on his bicycle rides. Responding to the Holy

Jimmy, the biker.

Spirit's guiding, I prayed even more fervently than usual.

It was a Thursday afternoon, and I was in our motorhome making last minute preparations for a trip involving our music ministry. We were just about to leave, when our son dropped by to tell us goodbye and to say that he would be praying for us. I took the opportunity to ask him if he ever rode his bike alone. With a big grin that said, *Mom, you worry too much,* he waved and was out the door. The rest of the day I fought my anxiety with pleas of protection for my son. I even smiled inwardly thinking, *Can't wait till HE has kids!*

My cell phone rang early the next morning. It was Jimmy. In a soft tone he said, "Mom? I'm OK, but I had a pretty bad accident on my bike yesterday." Not knowing just what "I'm OK," meant, my heart began to race as he told me the story.

Jimmy was riding his bike with his friends and happened to be the leader of the pack. When he came to a fork in the road, he called back, "Right or left?" He couldn't hear them when they said, "Right!" He turned left. When he realized they had gone the other direction, he began to pour on the speed to catch up. He topped a hill going about twenty miles an hour, when a very large dog came out of nowhere! Jimmy didn't slow down much because dogs would typically run alongside of the bike. This one didn't. It ran right out in front of him!

Upon impact, Jimmy felt himself being hurled over the bicycle's handlebars. Landing on his head, he hit the pavement in the middle of the street with a deafening thud! *Thankfully he was wearing a helmet!* Stunned, he lay on the road, unable to catch his breath. He began to see stars and hear birds singing when, all of a sudden, a man bent over him telling him not to move. Jimmy's vision was blurred, but he could make out the faces of his buddies standing around him. *Wow, I've really done it this time!*

Jimmy and his wife, Katelyn, with Zoie and Sonny.

"Is the dog all right?" Jimmy asked.

The man told him that the dog belonged to him and was OK. The man continued to plead with Jimmy not to move. He had seen Jimmy fly through the air. He had seen him land on his head and slide down the rough pavement. He was in total disbelief that Jimmy was conscious and talking. He was certain he would be dead! With cell phone in hand, the man was ready to call an ambulance.

In a matter of minutes, Jimmy's vision cleared, and he felt well enough to stand up. The man protested, but Jimmy knew he was lying on a yellow line in the middle of the road. Everyone assured him that they were standing in a circle around him so that he wouldn't get hit. The kind man offered to take Jimmy to the hospital to be checked out, or at the very least, take him home. But Jimmy refused, feeling that he was truly OK. The wheel of his bike was bent about an inch, and the seal on his helmet was broken, but he still managed to ride home!

When he got home, he called his doctor. Other than being very sore for the next few days, he sustained no serious injuries from the collision.

I truly believe that the devil was trying to destroy my son, but the Lord had prevented it. God, being all powerful, certainly did not need MY prayers in order to act on Jimmy's behalf, but by impressing me to pray, there was no doubt in my mind that God had performed a miracle in saving him. This miracle not only increased my faith in my heavenly Father, but it increased Jimmy's faith as well. The Lord proved His words to be true. He IS our Refuge and a very present Help in trouble. Don't leave home without Him!

Angel on the River

For He shall give His angels charge over you, to keep you in all your ways.
In their hands they shall bear you up,
lest you dash your foot against a stone. Psalm 91:11, 12, NKJV

Paddle right, paddle left!" The instructions from our friend rang out over the noise of the Ocoee River as my husband, Jimmy, and I encountered our first white water rafting experience. It was a beautiful Sunday afternoon when we put on our safety gear and climbed into the small rubber craft. As I sat in my assigned position, my thoughts carried me forward to the upcoming 1996 Olympics to be held in Atlanta, Georgia. The Ocoee River, near our home in Tennessee, was the site for the Olympic kayaking events. I was about to take a ride down an Olympic course designed for trained athletes! *I must be crazy,* I thought.

As we started our journey, our guide, who was also a friend of ours, would call out instructions telling us how and when to paddle. Each command helped guide us through the water. Suddenly, without warning, we hit some large rapids and without any warning, our raft was overturned! It was as if a large vacuum was sucking me down to the bottom of the river. My life jacket felt worthless as I struggled to kick and swim my way to the top. Looking up through the murky water, I could see the overturned raft above me. As I tried to surface, my head bumped the raft instead of breaking through to the air that my lungs were screaming for! Finally, when I didn't think I could hold my breath for another second, I broke through the surface of the river!

Jimmy had climbed on top of a rock in the middle of the river. He was frantically searching for me. As I surfaced, he reached out to grab me, but the current ripped me from his grasp. I knew I was in trouble. I was exhausted and could barely keep my head above the swirling water. To my far right was the riverbank. The current was so strong and I was so weak, there was no way I could swim across the current to the bank. To my left were huge, slick boulders that offered no way of escape. I was trapped. I began to pray, *Lord, if it is Your will that I die, it's OK because I belong to You. I trust You with my life. However, if it is not my time to go, I need Your help, NOW! Please!*

As I battled to keep my nose and mouth above the water, I saw a branch snaking across the surface of the river. As soon as I got close enough, I reached out and grabbed it, hanging on for dear life! "Thank You, God!" In a matter of seconds, however, I began to feel my hands slipping as the river tugged at my body. If I lost my grip, I would be hurled down the river to some waterfalls. If I got sucked under again, I was certain that I would lose my life. Once again, I cried out to my Savior.

At that moment, seemingly from nowhere, a man in a kayak appeared. "Hold on! I'm here to help!" he said.

How in the world is he going to get out of his kayak and help me? I wondered. We would both be in the same situation, plundering down the river toward the waterfalls. But before I knew it, I felt him behind me slipping his arms under mine. I felt myself being pulled back toward the slick, smooth rocks and then being lifted higher and higher until I was sitting about eight feet above the river. He was sitting next to me and I looked into his freckled face with disbelief. "How in the world did you get me up here?" I asked. There was absolutely no way he could have pulled me out of that river and perched me on that big rock. He gently smiled and spoke soothing words, but totally evaded my question. I asked him again and again, but each time he dodged the question.

Soon I saw Jimmy and our two friends coming down the river looking for me. Much to their relief, they saw me sitting on the rock above the river.

The man helped me to my feet and it was then that I realized that I was taller than he was! He pointed to a path that wound down to the river's edge where I could meet my husband and friends. As I started down the path, I turned to thank him . . . but he was gone! No man, no kayak . . .

nothing! It was at that very moment, I knew without any doubt, that my guardian angel had rescued me!

It took a long time before I could wrap my brain around what had happened! Every time I would try to talk about it, I would break down into tears. Then I began to doubt myself. I began to ask the Lord for some assurance that it *was* my guardian angel who had saved me from the raging river on that fateful day.

One day I was reviewing the story, and I mentioned the man who was sitting with me on the rock. "What man?" Jimmy asked. "I know about the man in the kayak who rescued you, but when I saw you on the rock, you were sitting alone!" God had answered my prayer! That was the assurance I needed. I thanked my God once again for His marvelous love and care.

Friend, I don't know what your guardian angel looks like, but mine appeared small in stature and had freckles. Freckles? It's amazing what one remembers! Nevertheless, you do have an angel and he is taking care of you just like mine did on the river that Sunday. The Scriptures say, "For He shall give His angels charge over you, to keep you in all your ways." I'm living proof of this glorious promise!

"Sugar, You've Got to Go!"

A happy heart makes the face cheerful. Proverbs 15:13, NIV

"There, Mr. Johnson, now you can enjoy the sunshine!" Deborah said to her patient as she parked his wheelchair on the patio of the nursing home. "I'll be back later, sugar, to check on you," Deborah promised in her darling southern accent.

If you met our daughter Deborah, your first impression of her would be that she was full of sweetness and cheerfulness. You would also find her to be one of the most caring people on the planet. She is also delightfully funny and lights up a room whenever she walks in!

Deborah graduated from Southern Adventist University with an RN and a bachelor's degree in long-term health care. One of requirements for her degree was to do an internship at a local nursing home facility. During that internship, she worked every area from the laundry room to management.

On one particular day, she was assigned to do laundry. The washer and dryer were heavy-duty machines, so she figured since they were so big and she was washing large loads of bulky linens, she must need a lot of detergent. After putting a huge load in the washer, along with way too much detergent, she left the laundry room, closing the door behind her. Deborah looked like a little doll that should be put on a shelf and admired! But in truth, she was smart, strong, and very capable.

When she came back to the laundry room, she saw detergent seeping out under the door. When she opened the door, to her horror, suds and water were everywhere! She was overheard saying, "Well I guess I just wasn't made to do laundry!" Everybody cracked up because she didn't know how to mop either. She says it's my fault because I never taught her how!

Everyone loved her. The staff admired her work ethic, the patients loved the TLC she gave them, and the director appreciated her professionalism. He called her into his office one day and praised her for all of her fine qualities. However, he had one major concern. "Deborah, as the director of a health care facility, I have the unpleasant task of firing people at times. You are so sweet and kind to everyone, how would you go about firing someone?"

"Well," she said, "I would just bring them into my office, ask them to have a seat, and say, 'Sugar, you've got to go!' " The director laughed so hard, he almost fell out of his chair!

Photo taken by Garrett Nudd

Carlton, Caroline, Josh, Deborah, and Adam Vollberg.

Deborah is now a grown woman and is married to a physician, Carlton Vollberg. They have given us three beautiful grandchildren: Caroline, Adam, and Josh. Deborah has used all of the wonderful qualities God blessed her with in raising her children and caring for her husband.

I'll never forget the day that her husband opened his new medical practice. He had just left Chattanooga's oldest medical group and took many of the patients with him. His opening day was a busy one with a heavy patient load. On top of that, a number of his patients just showed up to make sure he was still in Chattanooga! Many who didn't have appointments waited hours to see him. At one point, Carlton called Deborah and told her that the waiting room was full and most of the people had gone without food or water for many hours. He was very concerned. In no time at all, she showed up with boxes of lunch and bottles of water. Anyone listening could hear her asking, "Are you hungry or thirsty, *sugar*?"

When our Lord walked this earth, He loved every soul as if he or she were the only one on the planet. In the book The Desire of Ages, *Mrs. White wrote that as a child Christ would share His meager lunch or a cup of cold water with someone in need. He could be heard singing as He worked and brought joy and happiness to everyone who heard Him. When He began His ministry, He healed the sick, fed the hungry, and raised the dead. People from all walks of life loved Him and longed to be around Him. How about you, my friend? Do people smile and love to be around you? Does your life produce happy hearts and cheerful faces?*

Just the Right Hose

You called in trouble, and I delivered you. Psalm 81:7, NKJV

Pastor Kenneth Cox had invited my husband, Jimmy, and I to go to Arvada, Colorado, to help with music for a series of evangelistic meetings he was having. We were excited about being a part of this evangelistic outreach as we knew that many people would hear Bible truths for the first time. Dona Klein is a talented organist who always played for Pastor Kenneth's meetings, and Jimmy always enjoyed playing with her. They have similar styles on the piano and organ.

We were traveling in our motorhome, or coach, as we call it. It's easy to pack all the musical instruments and the PA equipment in the bays below, and, believe me, there are a lot of instruments. If you've ever seen my husband play, I can tell you, he's a regular "one-man band"!

Before we left, Jimmy checked the motorhome for any problems, as was his usual custom. Everything looked great! As my brother Ron said, "With a motorhome, you've always got problems. You just don't know what they are yet!" Unfortunately, as we soon found out, that was really true!

We started on our journey from Tennessee to Colorado, and we were making good time. We had just passed over the Kansas line into Colorado, when Jimmy said casually, "We should get there easily by this afternoon."

Seconds after uttering those words, the lights on the dashboard flashed on, indicating engine trouble. "I guess I spoke too soon," Jimmy smiled cautiously as he quickly pulled over onto the shoulder of the road and put on the flashing hazard lights.

He walked to the back of the bus where the engine was located, while I waited anxiously, wondering how serious the problem could be. I didn't have to wait long.

"We've blown a hose, and not just any old hose. It's a special one that's probably going to have to be ordered from the factory!"

"Oh no!" I heard myself say as the look of reality of what this meant swept across my face.

Here we were out in the middle of *nowhere,* stuck in a coach that would not run without this particular hose. We both went to our heavenly Father asking for help. He had always taken care of us before, and we had no doubt that He would now.

When we finished praying, Jimmy said, "I'll disconnect the van and go to the next exit to see what I can find. Are you OK staying with the coach, or do you want to go with me?"

I told him that I would be fine staying with the coach and not to worry. As he disconnected the van that we pulled behind our coach, I said another prayer as I watched him drive away. I then opened my Bible and began to read from the book of Psalms. I love how David expressed His praises for our heavenly Father, especially in times of need. I decided that was exactly what I needed to read at this very time of our trouble, and we definitely needed God's help!

I read several chapters and then turned to Psalm 81. When I came to verse 7, it said, "You called in trouble, and I delivered you." I couldn't believe my eyes! God was telling me He was going to help us! I got down on my knees, and with tears I thanked Him! Why is it that when I asked in faith, believing that He would help us, I was so surprised? Our God is *always* faithful!

It seemed like Jimmy was gone forever, as I watched the clock tick by, but pretty soon he pulled up in the van. I couldn't wait to show him what I read, and he was as surprised as I was.

"Well I didn't have much hope until you showed me that text," he said. "Let me explain."

Jimmy began to tell me what he'd been through. He went quite a distance on the freeway to get to the next exit. When he got off the exit, he saw two police cars parked nearby. He drove over to them and got out of the van. He explained our problem and asked if there was anyone in the area that might help us. They told him of a man who could possibly help and gave directions to his business. Jimmy got back in the van and followed the directions he was given.

After driving a long time, he came upon what looked like a mechanic shop. His heart suddenly sank. The building was dilapidated, dirty, and rundown. Bricks were missing from the walls, and old car parts were lying around the parking lot. *What was I thinking coming here? They're not going to be able to help me,* he thought. *Especially when I need such a specific item. Well, I'm here. I guess I might as well ask.*

He got out and went in. There were several men standing around talking. He told them his problem, and that the police had directed him here. The guys shook their heads and told him he was at the wrong place. They gave him another set of directions to the place where they thought a man could help.

Jimmy followed those directions and finally found the man. His name was Pete. He was just a down-home country fellow.

"I don't reckon I can help ya much, but I'm willin' to try if you want me to." The man wiped the grease from his hands on his already dirty overalls.

Most importantly, he was willing to work on the coach right where it was. We wouldn't have to tow it to his shop, which would have been extremely difficult to find a tow service and also very expensive. Jimmy gave explicit directions on how to find our motorhome.

"I'll be along shortly. I have something I need to finish up first," he said, turning to go back to his work.

It was little wonder why Jimmy had come back to the coach so worried. After I showed him the Bible text, Jimmy was encouraged, and we had another prayer thanking God for what He was doing.

As promised, it wasn't long before Pete drove up in his large flatbed work truck. To get to us, he had to go to the exit past us, go over the overpass, and get back on the interstate going the same direction we were. We were so thankful that he was willing to go to all that trouble, especially when he didn't even think he could fix it!

Jimmy met him at the back where the engine was. He shook his head. He said he could fix it, but he would need to find *just the right hose.* But where could we get *just the right hose* in the middle of nowhere? But wait a minute! Hadn't God already delivered us? We silently prayed for more faith!

Pete told us that the closest gas station was at the next exit. They carried a few hoses and even though he thought it was a lost cause, he was willing to check. Jimmy knew which gas station he was talking about, because he remembered seeing it when he had talked to the policemen.

Jimmy followed Pete to the gas station. He wanted to save the guy another trip, and he wanted to pay him for his trouble if, indeed, it was a lost cause. They walked inside and went directly to the wall display of hoses. Suddenly, Pete's eyes opened wide in amazement. "I can't believe it! This is it! This is it! The exact one!" he shouted.

Jimmy was ecstatic! The text was true! "You called in trouble, and I delivered you."

Pete had the coach fixed, and we were back on the road in no time at all. Jimmy told him who we were, and that we were on our way to help with some evangelistic meetings. We paid him extra for all of his trouble and gave him some of our CDs. Pete looked at us and shook his head, still in awe of what had just happened! He agreed that the Lord had been with us.

Dear friend, is your life broken down? Do you have more problems than blessings? Are you out of work, or are you sick? I don't have the solutions for you any more than I had the right hose for that coach! But Jesus does. Go to Him just as you are, and tell Him that you want Him to take over your life.

The Bible says in Philippians 4:6, 7, "Be anxious for nothing, but in everything by prayer and supplication, with thanksgiving, let your requests be made known to God; and the peace of God, which surpasses all understanding, will guard your hearts and minds through Christ Jesus" (NKJV). Won't you give Him your heart? You're safe with Him in control.

Exploding Glass

The LORD will keep you from all harm—he will watch over your life;
the LORD will watch over your coming and going
both now and forevermore. Psalm 121:7, 8, NIV

It was two o'clock in the morning when there was a loud boom and the house shook. My daughter Rondi and her husband, Mike, sat straight up in bed and looked at each other, asking the question, "What was that?" Their bedroom and bathroom were being repainted and redecorated, so they were sleeping downstairs in the family room on the sofa that made into a bed. Their infant son was upstairs asleep in his crib. They both bolted out of bed and went flying up the stairs.

When Mike and Rondi reached the main floor of the house, they were relieved that their son was fine, and sleeping soundly. Then they began to go from room to room searching for any clues as to what had caused all the commotion. Everything seemed to be fine, until they came to the door of their bathroom. The horror before them was unbelievable! The entire bathroom floor was covered in glass! There were big pieces and little slivers of glass several inches wide. The mirror over their vanity was large and extremely heavy. When the house was being built, the mirror was installed by the builders. It measured eight feet wide and went clear to the top of the high ceiling. It had been improperly installed, and so, in time, had become unstable, until it suddenly fell off the wall, exploding into a million pieces. The force was so strong that it cut up their stone floor!

Photo taken by Carrie Workman

Rondi and her husband, Mike, with Blake and baby Olivia.

Looking at the disaster before her, all Rondi could think of was that the mirror landed exactly where her infant son played while she took a shower everyday! She also began to think of the workers that had been in the bathroom painting, and her housekeeper who had been cleaning the mirror. Anybody that had been in that bathroom, including her and Mike, could have been cut to pieces! Pregnant with their second child, she suddenly felt faint and nauseated just thinking about what *could have been*!

I remember when my children were growing up, I would pray for them on a daily basis. I would ask the Lord to place a hedge of protection around them by surrounding them with their guardian angels. I remember thinking if I could just get them raised, I wouldn't have to worry over their safety as much. I was *so* wrong! Now I not only pray for their safety but my grandchildren's as well! Every day I ask God to continue to send His angels to protect them all from physical as well as spiritual danger. The devil is out to get them any way he can! In John 10:10, the Bible says, "The thief does not come except to steal, and to kill, and to destroy." I am so thankful that the verse continues with Jesus saying, "I have come that they may have life, and that they may have it more abundantly" (NKJV).

Rondi and Mike sank to their knees and thanked the Lord for protecting them and their baby from harm or death. They were also thankful that if the mirror had to come down, that it came down in the middle of the night when no one was working or cleaning.

There is a verse in the Bible that is very dear to my heart and has proven true to me on so many occasions. It says, "If you make the Most High your dwelling—even the LORD*, who is my refuge—then no harm will befall you, no disaster will come near your tent. For he will command his angels concerning you to guard you in all your ways" (Psalm 91:9–11, NIV). Oh, dear friend, if you don't know this to be true in your life, I invite you to get to know your Creator. Accept Him as your Lord and Savior and invite Him take over your being. Spend time with Him in His Word and talk to Him every day. With our lives safely controlled by His hand, we don't have to worry about the future. Our safety is in Him!*

The Greatest Physician

" 'I will restore health to you and heal you of your wounds,' says the LORD." Jeremiah 30:17, NKJV

"Mrs. Rhodes, I hate to tell you this, but your test results indicate that you have CREST syndrome." My doctor had a look of concern on his face.

"What in the world is CREST syndrome?" I asked.

He explained that CREST is an autoimmune disease and each letter in the name is an acronym for a symptom of the disease. It is a hard disease to diagnose and there is no known cure. It is not life threatening, but it can be painful to live with. I had already discovered that! I have small calcium deposits, like small rocks, in my joints. I can't kneel, and I can't rest my elbow on a table or an armrest, unless it is heavily padded. I have a red rash that covers my face, neck, and arms. But the very worst to deal with is the limited scleroderma that affects my limbs.

Several years ago when our two youngest children were still in college, we went on a family ski trip to Colorado. I grew up skiing in New Mexico as a kid, but it had been years since I had been on skis. But, just like riding a bike, it all came back, and I had a wonderful time keeping up with my kids, flying down the blue and black runs. Late in the afternoon, however, my rented ski boots were really beginning to hurt. My husband helped me get them off, and I discovered the boots had rubbed a painful hole in each shin! I didn't know at the time that I had CREST. The wounds took forever to heal and the scabs were tender to the touch and never went away.

I finally discovered wound care. After a very, very painful five months of weekly debridings and totally being off my feet, the wounds healed up. But the process had been awful. After each debriding session, which was when the doctor took tweezers and picked out any yellow in the wounds so that the blood could get through, he filled the wounds with a medication to aid in healing. The nurse would then bandage my legs from my feet to my knees and put compression stockings over the bandages. I would be in so much pain after each of these sessions that I would scream and cry. I would go back for my weekly appointment, and my wounds would look worse instead of better. The doctor finally realized that I was allergic to all of the medications he had used. The medicines had actually fried my skin, making the situation much worse! Finally, after a very long time, my wounds healed, and I was just thankful that ordeal was over! I still had no idea what was going on with my health.

One day I went to see a plastic surgeon about the rash on my face, neck, and arms. I was using more and more makeup to cover the rash and it seemed to be getting worse. Being on camera and singing for 3ABN was something I really enjoyed doing, but covering the rash was becoming more and more of a challenge. Several doctors had looked at it, but none knew what was wrong. So I made an appointment with a plastic surgeon, hoping he had a laser treatment that could remove it. The doctor's bedside manner lacked compassion, and he bluntly told me that he would not touch me. He said I had an autoimmune disease of some kind, such as lupus or scleroderma. He told me to see a rheumatologist. With that, he turned on his heel and left the exam room.

I sat stunned at what he had told me. I knew a little bit about lupus because of a dear friend who had it. But the only thing I knew about scleroderma was that it caused skin and internal organs to become hard, like wood, and the person affected died a long, painful, disfiguring death.

I blindly made my way to the car. I barely had time to shut the door before I burst into tears! I cried out to the Lord and begged for strength just to drive the forty minutes home. As I came out of the parking garage, I realized I was in the middle of a horrible rainstorm. The wind was unbelievable! It was all I could do to keep my car on the road! I was so distraught over the news the doctor had given me that I hardly noticed that

I was right in the middle of a tornado! All I can tell you is that my angel must have driven that car and gotten me home!

Our oldest daughter, Deborah, is married to a doctor, and as soon as I could, I got him on the phone and told him my horrible news! Bless his heart; he was so patient with me! He explained to me that there are two kinds of scleroderma and if I had systemic scleroderma, I would know it by now! He told me that I probably had CREST syndrome, which was very rare and very difficult to diagnose. I definitely needed to see a rheumatologist.

The rheumatologist ran some tests and, sure enough, I had CREST syndrome. He told me that it would be more annoying than deadly. He gave me medicines to clear up the rash and to prevent any more painful calcium deposits. I was allergic to all of the medications! I was so discouraged. But God had a plan. God *always* has a plan—we need only to ask! The Bible tells us in James 4:2, "You do not have because you do not ask" (NKJV). This is actually where my story begins!

We were in Alamogordo, New Mexico, helping our dear friend, Pastor Kenneth Cox, with an evangelistic series of meetings. I was nursing a new wound on one leg, and I was in a lot of pain. The doctor allowed me to make the trip as long as I kept my leg elevated as much as possible. Since I was allergic to the medicines, I did my own daily "wet to dry" wound care, with the doctor checking me weekly.

Every afternoon we would go to the church to prepare for the evening meeting. After selecting the songs and getting an audio check, I would take my place on the front pew and prop my leg up on a covered box and stay put until it was time for me to sing. I couldn't greet the people as I enjoyed doing, or chat with them to get to know them better. All I could do was sit, feel sorry for myself, and hurt! My prayers were filled with tears and self-pity.

I don't remember what I was doing when the idea popped into my head that I should be anointed! *That's what I need—an anointing service!* I thought. But then doubt began to creep in. *I'm not good enough to ask for healing. I'm so sinful that there's no way God would heal ME! And besides, I'm not on my deathbed!*

However, the Bible says, "The one who comes to Me I will by no means cast out" (John 6:37, NKJV). "Come to Me, all you who are weary and burdened, and I will give you rest" (Matthew 11:28, NIV). I was weary all right. Weary of the pain. Weary of dealing with a wound that was so deep I could see the tendon in my leg.

When Jesus walked the earth, He healed all who had the faith to ask Him. The Bible also says in James 5:14, "Is anyone among you sick? Let him call for the elders of the church, and let them pray over him, anointing him with oil in the name of the Lord" (NKJV).

I decided to ask Kenneth if it would be appropriate for me to have an anointing service. I wanted the pain to go away. I wanted the wound closed. But most importantly, I wanted to give many more years of service to my precious Lord and Savior.

I approached Kenneth with the idea, and he greatly encouraged me. He said we could meet with the whole team at the church and have the anointing before the meeting started. A kind of shyness came over me, and anyone who knows me knows that it's not in my nature to be shy! As much as I appreciated his gracious offer, I asked if it could be a bit more private with just him and our close friends, the Kleins, at our motorhome and, of course, Jimmy would be there as well. Gordon Klein was an ordained minister and Jimmy was an elder in our church. Dona Klein was one of the godliest people I knew and a dear, dear friend.

Kenneth was most agreeable and so were the Kleins. I was elated and felt that the Lord was going to do a wonderful thing to the glory of His name! But the devil was not about to let this whole thing go down unchallenged! For the first time in years, Dona came down with some kind of bug. It was so bad, she knew she would not even be able to play the organ for the meeting that night. For her to be too sick to play was unheard of! So she prayed for me from her sick bed.

In the living room of our motorhome, Kenneth, Gordon, and Jimmy knelt around me in a circle. Kenneth read from the Bible and placed some olive oil on my forehead. Then he prayed a sweet, simple prayer. Listening to him talk to God, I felt that he *knew* the Master personally and the Master *knew* him!

We all lingered a bit in the sweetness of the moment and then headed out the door for the meeting. When I got to the church, I noticed that my pain had eased—a lot! I stood and greeted the people. I was all over the church bubbling with happiness. I told no one anything, but I was feeling better!

I slept like a baby that night, and when I awoke the next morning, for the first time in a long time, I felt no pain! Before I took my shower, as was my routine, I removed the bandages. This was usually a very painful process because the wound, or hole as I called it, was packed with wet gauze the day before. By this time it had dried, sticking to the yellow protein that had to come out! As I would pull out the gauze, it would bring the yellow with it so the blood could reach the wound for healing. (My apologies to all the squeamish!)

Upon removing the bandages, the piece of gauze fell out. It had no yellow on it, and it was perfectly dry. I looked at the wound, and I couldn't believe my eyes! It was completely closed except for a tiny pinhole! I called out to Jimmy, and he came running.

"Am I seeing things?" I asked. Healing that normally took months happened overnight! Jimmy assured me that I was not seeing things. The wound was basically closed. Needless to say, we rejoiced and praised the Lord!

When we got home, I went to the hospital to see my doctor. His eyes nearly popped out of his head when he looked at the wound! He asked me what in the world I had done to bring on such healing. I told him about Kenneth and the anointing service. His response was, "I need him to come down here and pray over a whole bunch of people!"

What a miracle! What an incredible God! Dear friend, He wants to bring healing into your life as well. It may or may not be physical healing. It may be spiritual healing or emotional healing. Won't you ask Him today?

"I Will Restore You"

Heal me, O LORD, and I shall be healed; save me, and I shall be saved, for You are my praise. Jeremiah 17:14, NKJV

I listened to the still, small voice as I lay in my hospital bed . . . *"I will restore you."* I knew beyond a shadow of a doubt that the Lord was speaking to me. Was it an audible voice? No, but I knew God was speaking to my mind.

I had suffered a stroke due to uncontrolled blood pressure, and God impressed me that He would take care of me. It was going to be all right. I had the greatest Physician in the world at my bedside, and I had complete peace.

It all began on a Sunday night. We were busy as usual, doing the work God had given us to do. Jimmy and I had done a concert Saturday night and were looking forward to flying to California on Tuesday to work with Pastor Kenneth Cox and Pastor John Carter. I was sitting in a comfortable chair, feeling a bit tired. I said something to Jimmy, and I noticed I had a hard time talking. Thinking that I was just weary, I went to bed. The next morning, Jimmy had an early appointment, so he left before I got up. I had an appointment with my dentist to have my teeth cleaned. I quickly got ready and went to his office. With a mouth full of equipment, I didn't say much. When I left, however, I had difficulty talking. I got into the car and tried talking to myself all the way home. My speech was deteriorating fast!

When I got home, I called Jimmy. He couldn't understand very much of what I was saying, but he heard enough to know I was in trouble and came home right away!

Next, I called my doctor. The poor nurse didn't have any better time understanding me than my husband did. She tried hard to figure out what I was trying to say and then informed me that the doctor was on vacation and that I should go directly to the emergency room.

When Jimmy came home, I barely said two words, and he immediately called our son-in-law, Carl, who is a doctor. He told us to go immediately to the largest hospital in Chattanooga, as it is one of six hospitals in the U.S. that is known for having cutting-edge treatment in the area of stroke. Carl called ahead and they were waiting for me when I walked in the door!

The doctor ordered an EKG and then a CAT scan. I was wheeled into an area where there were curtains for privacy. My blood pressure registered at 200/100. Jimmy and I anxiously waited for the doctor for what seemed like . . . hours! Finally, he came in.

He stated that the CAT scan showed nothing and that he had no choice but to release me. Jimmy could hardly believe his ears! That was enough to raise his blood pressure! He looked right at the doctor and said, "Her blood pressure is 200/100, and she's completely unable to talk! What are we supposed to do?" The doctor said that we should see a neurologist and then he dismissed me.

We were both stunned! When we got into the car, Jimmy called Carl. He was furious when he heard what the doctor had said. It was pretty late by this time, so he told us to go home but to be in his office first thing in the morning. Bright and early the next day, he had a cardiologist and a neurologist lined up for me to see. He felt they were the best in Chattanooga. They quickly put me in a different hospital and did an MRI and located the stroke. It wasn't a clot but a bleeder due to my high blood pressure. While I lay in the hospital, the phrase, *"I will restore you,"* kept floating through my mind. I had complete peace. God is so good!

The doctors immediately began treatment to lower my blood pressure. By the time I was ready to be released, it had dropped dramatically. They made appointments for me to see a hypertension specialist, a speech pathologist, and an occupational therapist. I had a little weakness in my right hand. The doctors called it a "mild stroke" and said that we should allow six months for, hopefully, a full recovery.

We canceled everything we had booked for the near future, and I started working on getting well. I went to see the hypertension specialist, and he started me on a new medication and kept me on my old medication as well. It really worked and brought my blood pressure down to a normal level. I was seeing the speech pathologist and the occupational therapist twice a week. I was making rapid progress and giving God all the credit!

Then one day, out of the blue, I woke up with my eyes and face badly swollen. Also, my speech was dramatically and negatively affected. I called my hypertension doctor, and he pulled me off the medication and gave me another. I reacted to that medication and to everything he prescribed after that.

Again I cried out to the Lord and heard Him say, *"I will restore you."* It gave me the peace that I desperately needed. The doctors still needed to find a medication that I could tolerate, but I absolutely knew God would provide. All my friends and family were praying for me, and, oh, how I needed and felt those prayers!

Finally, my doctor told me there was one medication left to try. I got on my knees and pleaded, "Please, heavenly Father, don't let me be allergic to it!"

The doctor advised me to take only half the pill to start with. I took it and had another bad reaction.

Again I prayed, "Lord, did I hear You right? Did You promise to make me well again, or am I hearing things? Did I misunderstand You?"

At that moment, I was strongly impressed to take a quarter of a tablet. It worked! I had a small reaction, but it was something that my allergy medicine could take care of, and it really kept my blood pressure down. God had used my precious son-in-law to give me the help that I needed, and I knew with absolute certainty that my heavenly Father had taken care of me! Praise God, He is so good!

I can tell you that before the six months were over, I was completely restored. My speech is normal and so is my blood pressure. God's message in Jeremiah 30:17 has become very precious to me. It says, " 'For I will restore health to you and heal you of your wounds,' says the LORD" (NKJV). I can tell you, without a doubt, that promise was real for me.

How is your health? Are you struggling with some disease, or do you have a loved one who is? Place your trust in our precious Savior, and He will give you the strength you need to face even the worst possible situation. As much as I hated the stroke, I wouldn't change a thing. I clung desperately to God for everything, and, because of it, my walk with Jesus is even sweeter! If everything is going smoothly in our lives, it is easy to lean on self, but it is through our trials that we lean on Jesus!

Breath of Life

Now to Him who is able to do exceedingly abundantly above all that we ask or think, according to the power that works in us. Ephesians 3:20, NKJV

Oh no, I'm really in trouble now! I thought to myself. I could already feel my legs swell, as well as my ankles and feet.

We were parked in our coach at 3ABN and there was a lot of pollen in the air. Somehow I had gotten away without my air purifiers, which keep the air clean wherever I am. As described in the chapter "The Great Physician," I have an autoimmune disease called CREST syndrome. Any kind of swelling can cause wounds that are extremely hard to heal and require months of painful wound care.

We came home, and all the swelling went down. But just as I thought, it left me with a large wound on my ankle about the size of a silver dollar and almost as deep as the bone! It left two smaller ones as well. The pain was so intense that I was hospitalized. My precious husband went through the whole ordeal with me and was the best nurse in the world!

We had several concert dates lined up for the fall and were really looking forward to getting back to our music ministry. I had a stroke in February and had fully recovered, so I was excited about getting on the road again! But now this!

I cried to the Lord, "Isn't a stroke enough of a health issue for one year?" But both health issues were my fault. The stroke was brought on by blood pressure that was out of control. I took my medicine, but really didn't monitor my pressure. And, of course, there was the swelling and the purifiers that were left at home. Crying out to the Lord as if He had caused my health issues was venting and, because of His longsuffering and grace, He listened and forgave.

In the meantime, we headed back to 3ABN for fall camp meeting. Our dear friends John and Beverly Carter were going to be there and we were anxious to see them and hear Pastor Carter speak.

I felt the Lord impressing me to ask John to have an anointing service for me and he graciously consented. John Carter, Jim Gilley, Danny Shelton, my husband, Jimmy, and other friends, all took turns praying for me. I was so touched to think that they would each pray for me in such a loving and powerful way. It brought me to tears.

But much to my disappointment, there was no change in the wounds. Same pain, same horrible wounds. I had told them all that I wanted the name of the Lord glorified, regardless of the outcome. So I continued praising Him and thanking Him even though I didn't know what His plan was for my healing.

Because I am allergic to all the medicines they put in the wounds for healing, I get the best help from the hyperbaric oxygen machine, or, as it is called for short, HBO. It is truly the breath of life for me. It is a clear tank that I'm in for an hour and a half, breathing pure oxygen at a simulated ocean dive of thirty-one feet. Over the years, I have received so much extra benefit from this therapy, such as making the calcium knots in my arms smaller, doing away with any allergies to pollens, preventing horrible wounds, and building up my immune system like nothing else can.

I asked a nurse once if I could come down and use the hyperbaric machine when I didn't have a wound, just to boost my immune system to fight the CREST syndrome. I would be happy to self-pay.

She turned on her heel as she went out the door and said, "We're not a spa!"

So when the Lord impressed me to ask for permission to use the hyperbaric machine as a boost to my immune system, I couldn't believe it! I prayed, "Lord, is that really what You want me to do?"

I was to meet someone from the business office before I had my first treatment Monday morning for my current wounds. Since I was self-pay, I had to sign some papers and give them a check. The impression from the

Lord to make another request was so strong that I couldn't ignore it. So Monday morning, I sat in a chair rehearsing in my mind what I was going to say when a sharply dressed business woman briskly walked in. She was kind but definitely all business. I finally got up my courage and said, "May I ask you a question?"

"Sure," was her reply.

"If I came to you with a prescription from my doctor for HBO to treat my CREST syndrome, to build up my immune system even when I am wound-free, would you allow me to use the machine?" I searched her eyes for any sign of grace and mercy.

She cocked her head and said, "Sure. I don't have any business cards with me, but I'll send you one."

I couldn't believe it! God gave me much more than I had asked for. He had provided layers of healing instead of just healing one wound! I couldn't wait to call everyone that had prayed for me and tell them.

It reminded me of the text in Ephesians 3:20 that says, "Now to Him who is able to do exceedingly abundantly above all that we ask or think, according to the power that works in us." He certainly did more than I could think or ask! He is my awesome heavenly Father who takes very good care of me.

Because of sin, there will be suffering on this earth until Jesus comes to take us home with Him. But we don't have to fear, for God loves us with an everlasting love. He stands ready to come to our rescue and fight our battles. He knows the end from the beginning, and He knows what is best for us. All we need to do is trust Him with our pain, our sorrows, our burdens, and, yes, even our health! Jesus longs for us to depend on Him for our every need. He loves us so very much, and He does not wish for any of us to suffer. Come to Him today with all of your wounds and hurts. He will take care of you!

He Heard Her Cry

"Fear not, for I have redeemed you; I have called you by your name; you are Mine. When you pass through the waters, I will be with you; and through the rivers, they shall not overflow you." Isaiah 43:1, 2, NKJV

Ruth learned, at a very early age, to fully trust in Jesus. When she was only six years old, my in-laws, Mother and Daddy Rhodes, learned that Ruth, their youngest child, needed to have major surgery. Because of infection, one of her kidneys needed to be removed. Today, having a kidney removed is a serious surgery, even with all of the modern advances, but when Ruth was little, it was even more dangerous. Doctors back then didn't have the medical knowledge, procedures, and medications that they do today.

Needless to say, the whole family was in prayer. Verses from the Bible that spoke of God's love and protection were read and quoted. With Jesus in her heart and a praying family and community close by, little Ruth went through the surgery without any complications. My husband, Jimmy, adored his baby sister and she adored him. As worried as he was, he knew she was going to be fine when he went into her room after the surgery and in her sedated condition, without opening her eyes, she told him to "Scram!" In her pain and fight to recover, that was probably as nice as she could be!

Many years later and now a grown woman, Ruth and her husband decided to take a vacation to Priest Lake, Idaho. They rented a condo on the lake and made the beautiful drive up from southern California. Spring was in full bloom, and there was lots of wildlife. They enjoyed the local ambiance and even stopped to have some locally made huckleberry pie. The sun was shining, and there wasn't a cloud in the sky. It was a perfect day for fishing, or so her husband thought!

After settling into their condo, they made their way to the marina where they rented a twelve-foot fishing boat that had a small engine. Ruth did not care about fishing and was fearful of the water, but it was a beautiful day, and she had plenty of reading material, so she thought she would be fine.

Ruth settled back in the little craft and enjoyed the sun and the water slapping gently on the sides of the boat. Suddenly, seemingly from nowhere, a mighty wind began to blow. The sun disappeared behind thick, ugly, black clouds. Soon the boat was being engulfed by six-foot waves. The motor sputtered and choked and then quit all together. No amount of effort was going to make it start again, and the only option left was to try and guide their boat back to shore . . . with a small wooden paddle!

"Put on your life jacket!" Ruth's husband yelled over the deafening noise of the storm. Ruth hung on for dear life as she watched the huge swells wash over their boat. With unbelievable fear and trembling, she lifted her face toward heaven and began to cry out to God. "Please, Lord, save us! Don't let us drown!"

Ruth continued to pray like she had never prayed in her life. She knew their lives were in danger and Christ was their only hope of survival! Verses that her parents had taught her as a child began to drift through her mind. "I can do all things through Christ who strengthens me" (Philippians 4:13, NKJV). "The angel of the LORD encamps all around those who fear Him, and delivers them" (Psalm 34:7, NKJV). "God is our refuge and strength, a very present help in trouble" (Psalm 46:1, NKJV). "In my distress I cried to the LORD, and He heard me" (Psalm 120:1, NKJV).

When Ruth opened her eyes, she couldn't believe what she saw. A beach! And it was close enough that if they got into the water and swam while hanging on to the boat, they could reach land. A short time later, exhausted, drenched, and shivering with cold, they crawled onto the shore . . . safe and sound!

Once they were able to catch their breaths, Ruth prayed again. "Lord, we need shelter from this storm!" Her prayer had barely escaped her lips, when she looked around and right before them was an old abandoned cabin! With thankful hearts, they huddled together inside their refuge, praising God for His loving care. They even found wood and were able to build a fire and dry out their clothes. What an awesome God, who provided for their every need!

The next morning dawned with a bright blue sky and calm waters. However, their next challenge was to figure out just how they were going to get back to the mainland.

The small engine on the boat still would not work. Priest Lake was huge, and they weren't sure anybody even knew they were missing. They were stranded!

Ruth and her husband, Dean, with Chester (on Ruth's lap) and Beauregard.

Again, Ruth went to the Lord in prayer. "Lord, please let someone find us! Please send help!" They began to look for any boat that might come close enough to hear their pleas for help. They didn't have to wait too long before Ruth spotted one. Jumping up and down, Ruth and her husband waved their arms wildly until they got the attention of the boaters. God had answered her prayers. Oh, what a praise report they had to share when they returned home! Ruth also had a prayer of thanksgiving to God for His faithfulness, grace, and mercy!

A question I have asked many times is, How do people get through this life without the Lord? There are so many fearful things happening in this world that just turning on the news can be a very scary thing to do. Storms of every kind are raging. Our Savior longs to save us and help us if we would just call on Him. He has been called the hound dog of heaven because He looks for us and pleads for us to let Him into our lives. Ruth wondered if anyone knew that they were even missing. Just recently, she shared this story with someone who lives near Priest Lake, and that person's response was, "That was you?" Many people had been looking for them, and amazingly she remembered it years later!

Jesus is looking for you! He wants you to be in heaven with Him. In fact, He loves you so much, He can't imagine heaven without you! Won't you give Him your heart today?

Saved From Death

In my distress I called upon the Lord*,*
and cried out to my God; He heard my voice from His temple,
and my cry came before Him, even to His ears. Psalm 18:6, NKJV

"What is this?" my husband asked himself as he lathered up for a routine shave before work. With his fingertips, he felt a small nodule in his neck. Unlike a lot of men, my husband is good about going to the doctor. The doctor felt the nodule and said it was nothing, but after he found a second nodule, he ordered a biopsy. Our son-in-law, Carlton Vollberg, is a physician, and he told Jimmy that it was probably nothing but encouraged him to have the biopsy just to be on the safe side.

The biopsy came back positive, and the doctor said it had to be surgically removed, along with the thyroid gland. He felt it was routine and not life threatening in the least. Afterward, there would be no chemotherapy or radiation. The surgeon was considered an expert in this field and, in fact, performed about five to seven of these surgeries a week.

Along with our children, I breathed a sigh of relief! I hated it that Jimmy had to go through the whole ordeal, but I was thankful that it wasn't life threatening. However, Jimmy didn't share my feelings. He had never had a health problem in his life. He had always had an unusual amount of energy and would ride his bike eighty miles without breaking much of a sweat! This news was devastating to him. It didn't matter how much encouragement he got, he did not have a peace about his upcoming surgery.

One day, while reading his Bible, Jimmy looked up the text in James 5:14, where it says that if anyone is sick, the elders of the church should be called and the person should be lifted up in prayer and anointed with oil. He asked me what I thought about having an anointing service, and I felt if it would give him some peace, we should have the service. So we met with our pastors, the head elder, and our children. The service was sweet and encouraging but, most importantly, Jimmy finally had peace.

The next morning Jimmy was rolled into surgery. It lasted about four hours and there were no surprises. Everything went as planned. He spent one night in the hospital and was released the next day.

When we arrived home, I made sure Jimmy was OK to walk in on his own. I walked just a step or two ahead of him with my arms full of his things. I unloaded my burdens on the kitchen counter and then stepped around the corner to check on some painting that was being done in the den. Suddenly, I heard this choking, gasping sound. I turned around just in time to see my husband falling. I immediately ran to him and managed to help him land on the sofa. I looked into his face. His skin was gray and ashen. His eyes were fixed. He was dying!

It didn't even cross my mind to perform CPR or call 911. All I could do was put my hands on his shoulders and scream for him to breathe! Suddenly, he blinked his eyes, took in a big breath, and woke up. As we sat there trying to get a grip on what had just happened, Jimmy told me that he had cried out to Jesus to save him. His cry was not audible, so I hadn't heard him, but praise the Lord . . . God heard him!

After a couple of days, Jimmy went back to the office. He insisted he was OK, although I wasn't convinced. I felt it was too soon for him to return to work. On Sabbath, our children and grandchildren came for dinner. I felt it would be good medicine for him to have everyone around. That morning Jimmy had complained of pain in his legs. I shared this with Carlton, and he immediately began checking for signs of a blood clot. After a quick evaluation, he took Jimmy to the hospital immediately!

Upon arriving, Carlton ordered an ultrasound of Jimmy's legs. The test showed a blood clot in each one. Then, because Jimmy had complained of labored breathing, Carlton ordered a CAT scan of his lungs. That test showed FIVE pulmonary embolisms! Just one can kill a person!

Jimmy was rushed into the ICU, and it just so happened that one of the best pulmonary specialists in the area was in the hospital on that Saturday night. He treated him for eight days and during that time Jimmy did a great deal of reflection. It is easy to be so busy doing the Lord's work that we forget who we are working for! It was through this experience that God impressed Jimmy to slow down and focus more on his Creator than on the many tasks at hand.

As we looked back on the whole ordeal, we could see the hand of God covering and protecting Jimmy. The Lord knew the experience we were going to have, and in His mercy, He provided that sweet prayer service to strengthen us for what was ahead. What an incredible blessing it is that we can always call upon Jesus and He will hear us!

How about you? Are you so busy doing good things that you don't have time to spend with the Lord? Doesn't make much sense, does it? Nothing we do is any good without Him!

Turn Your Eyes Upon Jesus

Draw near to God and He will draw near to you. James 4:8, NKJV

With the freshness and the beauty of the forest around him and the sound of the stream gently babbling at his feet, Adam could sense the presence of the Lord. God's warmth and peace flooded his soul. Adam, my seventeen-year-old grandson, was on his senior retreat. Camping in the mountains with his class, it was a perfect time and place to find the Lord.

They left the academy at noon on Tuesday, full of anticipation of the week ahead. When they arrived, they walked a mile, picked up their supplies, and set up camp. They had to do their own cooking, so the first thing on the "to do" list was to build a campfire. Each day they followed the same schedule, which was breakfast, then worship, followed by a class of some kind, such as "Survival in the Wild." This was followed by an activity that created trust among the kids—something that would draw them closer as a team. For example, one of the students would fall backward from a certain height and depend on the rest of the group to catch him or her. The whole activity was about trusting friends and ultimately finding a trusting relationship with God. The day would end with dinner and worship by the campfire.

Photo taken by Garrett Nudd

Adam.

On Sabbath, the counselor dispersed the

group to have their own worship. Adam made his way to a quiet spot in the woods. It was there that he knew God was with him. The verse in James 4:8 that says, "Draw near to God and He will draw near to you," became very real for Adam. He gave his heart anew to Jesus and prayed that he wanted to do whatever God wanted. Nothing else mattered but that he follow God's plan for his life.

That evening the students gathered for worship around the campfire. Many of the kids acted different, and their attitudes showed that a real change had taken place. The presence of the Holy Spirit was keenly felt.

Suddenly, storm clouds began to gather. Thunder started to boom and the wind began to blow. But just as Jesus calmed the angry sea so long ago, the wind stopped, the thunder silenced, and the clouds rolled back revealing a beautiful, calm night sky and a gorgeous moon! Jesus was about to be glorified around the campfire!

Many of the students had a real encounter with the Lord and were ready to share what Jesus had done for them. One after another got up and gave their testimony. They had given their hearts and lives to Christ. Their old habits of alcohol and partying were going to be a thing of the past. They wanted to keep their eyes on Jesus.

Adam was amazed! He knew there was a difference in these kids. He knew how wild they were, and he knew of the drugs and alcohol that took center stage in their lives. God began to impress him of the need to have something spiritual when they got back. Maybe something like a Bible study where they could continue their closeness with Jesus.

Adam began to ask some of his classmates, and the kids were all excited about getting together to study and get closer to the Lord. Fifty kids came to his first Bible study along with three faculty members! There were the same amount or more at subsequent Bible studies!

On Sunday morning, the last day of the retreat, one of the counselors was laying in his hammock when he heard a loud boom. He said it was just as if the devil had been kicked out of the camp! There was no doubt that Satan had been kicked out of a lot of hearts and lives during the retreat.

It's truly just like the old song says, "Turn your eyes upon Jesus, / Look full in His wonderful face, / And the things of earth will grow strangely dim, / In the light of His glory and grace." Just as the kids turned to Jesus, suddenly the attractions of this old world weren't so attractive anymore.

I've experienced that in my life too. The more time I spend with the Lord, the things that seemed so important to me in the past just don't hold my attention anymore. It's not something that I have to work at. It just naturally happens. What about you? Have you turned your eyes upon Jesus?

Photo Gallery

◄ *My family in 1958. From left: Mom, Pam, Dad, Carol Blake, and Ron on Dad's lap.*

◄ *My parents, Blake and June Chanslor.*

Photo shoot for Pam and Jimmy's album, You're Walking Down Sunshine Lane. ►

Jimmy Rhodes—a one-man band!

◄ *A little more sophisticated, but still a one-man band!*

Jimmy's parents, Truma and Ohlen Rhodes.

◀ *Our wedding.*

Our children, Jimmy, Rondi, and Deborah, when they were younger. ▶

Photo taken by Nicole Warren

Pam and Jimmy at 3ABN.

Josh, Caroline, and Adam Vollberg.

Our son-in-law and daughter, Dr. Carlton and Deborah Vollberg.

Photo taken by Garrett Nudd

Our son Jimmy and his wife, Katelyn.

◄ *Our grandson, Blake Oswald.*

Our granddaughter, Olivia Oswald. ►

Our son-in-law, Mike, and daughter, Rondi, with their children, Blake and Olivia Oswald.